Friday 14ᵗʰ Dec 1962

GROWING
Perpetual-Flowering
CARNATIONS

BAILEY'S SUPREME

Light salmon pink with high crown, this is an excellent
grower with strong erect stems

GROWING
Perpetual-Flowering
CARNATIONS

STEVEN BAILEY

With Foreword by
PERCY THROWER

SECOND EDITION

THE GARDEN BOOK CLUB
121 CHARING CROSS ROAD
LONDON W.C.2.

First published 1951 by
Ernest Benn Limited

Second impression 1954
Second revised and enlarged edition 1962

© *Steven Bailey 1962*

Printed in Great Britain

Foreword

by PERCY THROWER, N.D.H.

PERPETUAL-FLOWERING carnations have greatly increased their popularity since the war, and more and more people are growing the carnation, a truly magnificent flower.

Steven Bailey has been one of the most prominent exhibitors of these popular flowers for many years. His exhibits have been admired by thousands of visitors to the larger flower shows up and down the country. Apart from being an exhibitor, he is a first-class grower, and is responsible for the raising of many of our up-to-date varieties of today. With more than thirty years' experience in growing this one particular flower, he has worked in nurseries in Holland, Belgium, France and Denmark, as well as in this country. It is only by travelling such as this that one is able to learn all the various aspects of specialised growing.

How nice to see a book written by someone with such an experienced background as Steven Bailey—a valuable help to all who love and grow carnations. In this book Mr. Bailey tells us about the growing of carnations in such detail as can be plainly understood by even the beginner. Paragraph by paragraph we are taken through the various operations of growing either from seed or cuttings; potting, watering, stopping and other important points which if carefully followed cannot help but make us successful with our growing. Insect pests and diseases, the humbug of all we gardeners, are plainly dealt with, and we are given a month by month guide on the work we should be doing.

This valuable and instructive book will be of interest and assistance to all who grow carnations.

Contents

CONTENTS

Acknowledgements

Plates 12B, 13B and 14B are reproduced by
courtesy of Plant Protection Limited, and 14A
by courtesy of Imperial Chemical Industries.

List of Plates

Illustrations in Text

Introduction

PROMPTED BY the many conflicting views on the skill, knowledge and experience, as well as the 'special' soils and greenhouses required for successful growing of P.F. Carnations, I will endeavour to explain in simple language the 'Culture of the P.F. Carnations'.

My idea is to instil confidence and give encouragement to those who have always wanted to try a few plants for simple enjoyment and pastime after admiring the wonderful exhibits at various horticultural shows.

I do not say that it is as simple as all that to grow specimen blooms suitable for the show bench, nor could I explain in a few simple words the method of cultivation and the experience necessary to attain a perfection, which has taken me almost a lifetime to acquire.

But to grow a few plants, say anything from a dozen to fifty or even a hundred plants, and derive an unlimited amount of pleasure from doing so, is within the reach of everyone, and with this in mind I have written these notes.

However beautiful the Border Carnation, the Pink or any other member of the Dianthus family may be, none holds that charm and exhilarating beauty which the P.F. Carnation possesses.

Surely there is great beauty in the Border Carnation, the tiny Dianthus Alpine or even the common Sweet William (*Dianthus Barbatus*). In their correct setting they enhance any garden or rockery.

But what cheer a P.F. Carnation can bring during the sombre and dreary winter days when one enters a greenhouse, however small, filled with these plants in full flower—especially when they are the newer varieties with their splendid habit, long erect stems, and with such a wide range of colour in their so well formed blooms.

Since the introduction of the variety WILLIAM SIM, which came over from the U.S.A. around the year 1947, the standard of carnations has changed a good deal. This variety and its

1

'sports' can be found the world over in commercial establishments as well as amongst amateur growers. I have never known any variety to have made such an impact on any culture of flowers in the many years I have been associated with the growing of carnations, and the sports which have resulted from the variety WILLIAM SIM are too numerous to mention.

It is claimed that the present-day P.F. Carnation originated from a bush perpetual-flowering strain found amongst *Dianthus Caryophyllus*. Almost everyone knows that the carnation is frequently referred to as the 'Divine' flower, but this is equally true of the Sweet William or any of the many species of the genus Dianthus.

The carnation is a very ancient flower known for centuries before the Christian era. It was a native in the temperate regions of Europe and Asia and to a lesser extent of North Africa. It was common in France and Italy. Botanically, all carnations are referred to as *Dianthus Caryophyllus* although 'Caryophyllus' is but one of several hundred species of the genus Dianthus and there are a great many races and classes of carnations. A detailed study of this subject is very complicated and more than a little confusing.

I will therefore not bore the reader with all the data which I have read and found in the earliest reports on our subject but will report briefly what generally are the accepted facts.

The P.F. Carnation owes its origin to at least two Dianthus species, namely *Dianthus Caryophyllus* and *Dianthus Sinensis*. The history of this type is reputed to have begun in the city of Lyons in France about 1830. Centuries of hybridization and interbreeding produced new species and fixed types. During the early part of the 19th century, the Remontant Carnation was produced in France. This type was winter-flowering and produced blooms of greater substance. It is claimed that a well-known French gardener, Monsieur Dalmais was mainly responsible for its creation. Stocks of these carnations were eventually produced and were imported into the United States during 1852 and the first American variety was introduced in 1858. A well-known American variety was raised from these French originals and was named DAYBREAK. In 1895 Mr. Peter Fisher, then one of the leading American pioneers, raised the famous variety MRS. T. W. LAWSON by crossing DAYBREAK with a continental variety named VAN LEEUWEN. MRS. T. W. LAWSON was truly perpetual and its strong habit of growth compensated for a lack of form in its large cerise and serrated flowers.

In the meantime stock from France had been sent to England as well as some of the latest seedlings of the American varieties, and some of our leading growers very soon produced some remarkable seedlings such as WINTER CHEER, a bright scarlet, MISS JOLIFFE, pale rose, and others. The American seedling MRS. T. W. LAWSON also came to England and a well-known raiser of that time, Mr. Alfred Smith, crossed LAWSON with WINTER CHEER and produced the famous variety BRITANNIA, a scarlet.

It can justly be claimed that BRITANNIA was the forerunner of many famous British varieties. Equally famous American varieties would be ENCHANTRESS, SPECTRUM, TOPSY and several others which contributed in many respects to the advance in breeding in subsequent years.

Amongst the British raisers, the greatest must surely be the late Carl Englemann, a German immigrant to this country who finally established the world-wide known establishment at Saffron Walden in Essex; the late Montague Allwood, affectionately known by his many friends as 'Monty,' who together with his two brothers, George and Edward started and controlled his famous nurseries in Wivelsfield, Sussex, until his death in 1959; and to a lesser extent, the firm of Messrs. Stuart Low of Enfield, Middlesex.

Carl Englemann raised varieties such as the outstanding LADY NORTHCLIFFE which although only of medium size was the favourite of many commercial growers, due to its abundant production and good keeping qualities; SAFFRON—which was introduced in 1916 and was the best yellow I can remember; CUPID—(1920) a rosy salmon of good size; DORCAS—the crimson which was awarded the George Monro Cup in London in 1927.

Some of the best I remember from Monty Allwood, are WIVELSFIELD WHITE (1915), ROBERT ALLWOOD—a large bright scarlet, MARY ALLWOOD—(1913), WIVELSFIELD CRIMSON which are only a few of the older varieties. There were, however, dozens of new varieties arriving each year, for the chances of improvement were great in comparison with the opportunity we have today of creating something worthwhile with the standard we have now reached.

BARONESS DE BRIENEN must certainly be mentioned as one of the earliest and best known of the achievements of Messrs. Stuart Low & Co. It was a beautiful and very large shell pink which unfortunately was best in summer. This variety came out in 1912. EILEEN LOW was another from their Enfield nursery, whilst I think the most famous must be the clear large white— WHITE PEARL; the variety which was the favourite of King George V and which His Majesty frequently wore as a button-hole.

Another famous variety was LADDIE and its sport RED LADDIE raised in America and imported and introduced by Carl Englemann.

During the period 1915–1920 the carnation was often referred to as the 'American Tree Carnation.' No doubt this was due to the fact that at that time the new Perpetual Hybrids coming over from the U.S.A. possessed a taller habit and, being truly perpetual, were often grown for three or four years as a commercial crop, during which time they attained 5ft. to 6ft. in height.

It is often our experience when attending to our specialised groups of carnation blooms at shows all over the country, to hear remarks passed by one or another admirer; 'I wish we could grow a few of these, but then, we have no special heating in our greenhouse.' Or again: 'I have had a go but it was no use.'

When tempted to enter such conversation it has often been most difficult to explain that it is only a moderate and certainly not a high temperature that is needed, nor a specially-constructed greenhouse, but any ordinary small, or even home-made little place in which the finest plants could be grown.

I tell my listener that a temperature of say 40–45°F. is all that is needed, and if in summer, adequate ventilation to the top as well as the side of the greenhouse can be given, there should be no reason why he should not be able to grow quite good plants with the most pleasing results.

We have proved for ourselves that the old idea of high and lofty houses are not the only suitable carnation houses, and I know of at least one very experienced commercial grower who would tell you that he grows most remarkable crops in really small and low houses such as are normally used for cucumbers on commercial nurseries.

The aim should be to learn and understand the requirements of the carnation plant, and the better acquainted one becomes with these facts the more enthusiatic one will be.

Step by step we will now go over the most important points of general cultivation and care of the plant. I shall make my explanations as simple as possible and not too complicated as this book is intended to be a useful reference for the real beginners as well as the well-experienced.

We shall leave all the intricate matter for a later day when a beginning has been made and general routine work in carnation growing is progressing nicely.

1. *The Greenhouse*

AS ALREADY mentioned, the most simply constructed greenhouse is suitable, provided it is fitted with adequate ventilation —top as well as both sides of the house if it is of the span type, and at one side of a lean-to.

As carnations require all the light possible, especially during the winter when days are short and often dull, the structure of the house should not be too clumsy if built of timber, and the rafters should be spaced at least sufficiently apart to take a pane of glass 18in. wide.

Wherever possible, my preference would always be for sheets or panes of glass 24in $\times$ 24in. The rafters would be spaced approximately 24in. apart and there would be a lesser number of overlaps, all of which tends to make the house lighter.

Whilst speaking of overlaps I would like to emphasise this point more fully. It is common belief that the greater the overlap we give by overlapping one pane of glass over the lower one, the less chance there will be for drip. This, however, is a mistaken idea. I would never allow more than $\frac{1}{4}$in. Not only is this adequate but it avoids dust and algea collecting between the two sheets of glass which besides looking unsightly is detrimental to hygiene. Fungi collect at such places and furthermore it causes unnecessary shade which is not beneficial to the plants, especially carnations which after all enjoy all possible light, particularly during the winter months.

The best span roof would have a pitch of approximately 33 degrees. A 6in. wide $\times$ 1$\frac{1}{4}$in. ridgeboard with a glazing groove along each side is standard pattern. Rafters such as are used by commercial growers are 3in. $\times$ 1$\frac{1}{2}$in. with a $\frac{1}{4}$in. glazing groove or rabbet each side. The end rafters are usually of heavier timber but 3in. $\times$ 3in. would be sufficient.

I would insist on fixing a standard capping horizontally on the ridge which will protect the ridgeboard and at the same time cover the hinged edge of the roof ventilators. The capping

7

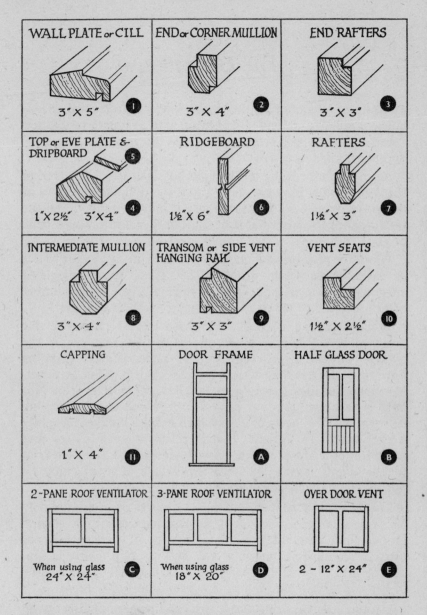

FIG. 1 Prepared and moulded timbers required for the construction of a greenhouse

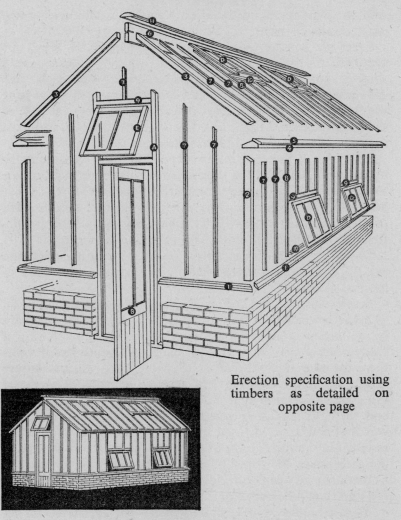

Erection specification using
timbers   as   detailed   on
opposite page

FIG. 2 An ideal carnation house.

should not be too wide and 3in. or 4in. × ¾in. thick would be
all that is needed.

Roof ventilators are obtainable in standard size. If the glass
size which is intended for use is 18in. × 20in., the standard
ventilator will be so made that it will take three such panes
giving an opening of approximately 5ft. × 20in. If, however, a

24in. × 24in. pane is decided on a roof vent taking only two panes should be used.

Even the smallest greenhouse should have at least one ventilator on each side of the ridge. For the longer house, I suggest roof ventilators placed alternately along each side. This in actual fact would mean that between each three pane ventilator there are three fixed panes of glass, or in the case of the larger pane and using a two-pane ventilator only, two fixed panes between each ventilator spaced along the roof.

The sides of the greenhouse, depending on its size, must be at least half glass and the remainder of solid construction. The lower part could be made of timber, asbestos or brick. To give adequate headroom along the eaves one should aim for 2ft. of solid construction, of which the best is brick on a 3in. × 9in. foundation and 4ft. of glass. This to my mind is ideal.

The brick sides having been erected, a timber wallplate 5in. × 3in. of the conventional pattern is placed on a bed of mortar.

Besides this we need corner mullions, intermediate mullions, in between which the side ventilators are placed. Side vents are by no means a superfluous item. Even when purchasing a ready-made greenhouse, always insist that besides roof vents there are also side ventilators to every 10ft. of greenhouse length on both sides. Do not accept the manufacturer's or salesman's assurance that side vents are not really necessary and therefore 'his' firm never fits them. During winter they would of course not be used but believe me they are absolutely essential in summer. Do not be tempted to make do by leaving the greenhouse door open as an alternative to side ventilators. I do not like an open door, it causes a draught directly over the soil and should be avoided.

We also require an eave plate which is the horizontal timber in between which and the wallplate the rafter and mullions are nailed. The underside of the eave plate should have a glazing groove for glazing the sides. Finally, we must not omit the drip bar.

For all construction work always use galvanised nails and brass screws. True, it will add slightly to the cost, but I would never be tempted to economise by using ordinary wire nails or steel screws. Invariably, such nails or screws will after a time start to rust, and consequently, rot will start in the timber around them. It has been my experience that galvanised or 'sheradised' nails, brass or 'sheradised' screws do prolong the life of the greenhouse and are well worthwhile.

We shall need a few extra lengths of rafter for the ends and either one or two half-glazed greenhouse doors with door-frames, depending on whether a door at one end or both ends is required.

Before starting building work I would treat all timber with green Cuprinol (SQD) and a double application is worth every effort and expense. Since 1944 I have treated all my timber with this material and the condition of my commercial greenhouses speaks for itself.

For glazing use a good linseed oil putty and ¾in. brass brads.

Timber constructed, of course, described only one kind of glasshouse. Much can be said in this respect for the modern metal-framed greenhouses, either in steel or aluminium, as the framework is so light all possible light is admitted; but in purchasing this type one should make sure it is provided with the sufficient ventilation, I mentioned earlier. I have, in my travels, seen many of these metal-framed houses at horticultural shows and elsewhere, and there are some in which the ventilation has been somewhat overlooked. They are, in my opinion, not suitable for P.F. Carnation growing. While on the subject of metal houses I would like to venture on to some dangerous ground by saying that, although it is argued that these houses are much colder than wooden structures, I personally do not think that the difference is so great as to be detrimental. If one considers the great surface of glass on a glasshouse compared with the actual surface in square inches of metal or wood where heat loss can occur, it would readily be seen that the heat loss through the glass is very great and that the little difference in metal or wood surface would be of small consequence. Personally I would not have any objection to a metal house for that reason alone. An aluminium glasshouse would be my particular choice.

Another point worth mentioning regarding metal houses, and which should be carefully noted when inspecting such a house with the intention of making a purchase, is that with some structures of this type there are colossal apertures

between the overlaps of the glass. It is very important to avoid
these for two reasons; one is that there is a considerable loss
of heat in cold weather as well as draughts, and secondly,
should we be troubled with pests as no doubt we shall at some
time or another, these houses do not lend themselves to the
use of the present-day smoke generators or fumigants as the
loss of the fumes would be so great as to make it impossible
to build up the required concentration.

These are a few points which have struck me after careful
inspection of show models and one should take them into
consideration when deciding to buy.

2. *Heating*

A REGULAR temperature maintained in one's greenhouse is
definitely a requirement which must not be overlooked.
Many are the forms of heating apparatus now on the market
for the amateur greenhouse; paraffin heaters are quite suitable
providing they do not emit fumes or smoke.

For a greenhouse say, 50ft. × 15ft. or more, a small boiler
such as the Robin Hood, the Ideal, and many other makes, is
the most usual, but of course regular attention must be paid
to the cleaning of the fire—seven days each week as well as
filling every night, which sometimes is not so convenient.

For an amateur's greenhouse, from the smallest to the
largest, I would choose an electric heater, thermostatically
controlled, which, I feel, would be the ideal. One could set
the thermostat at the required temperature and nothing further
need be done. When the temperature in the house rises above
the predetermined degree the thermostat cuts off and no fuel
or current is used, but as soon as the temperature drops below,
the heat is switched on and so a regular temperature is maintained. There is, however, one danger which in some districts
can be troublesome, and that is the cutting of the current at the
main due to power failure or a service breakdown. Fortunately,
repairs are quickly effected and taking my own location I

could not say that because of this possibility I would hesitate to consider such an installation.

A more recent revelation in greenhouse heating is hot air heating. Such a system appeals to me in particular for carnations. The air from the greenhouse is drawn in by means of a fan and passed over an electric grid which heats the air from where it is conducted through perforated polythene tubing. This tubing can be hung overhead or along the walls wherever it is required. Here again this system is completely thermostatically controlled as far as heating is concerned. The fan, however, can be manually controlled if desired and can be used for air circulation alone. This is a great advantage during the summer, and helps a good deal to avoid stagnation and thereby fungi infection such as mildew, botrytis, etc.

With solid fuel boilers, of course, the boiler has to be stoked and attended to during the entire twenty-four hours and fuel consumption is continuous. Many commercial growers have changed over to oil-fired boilers. These are more or less automatic and the control is by thermostat; only occasional attention is required providing, of course, there is an adequate supply of oil fuel in the tank. A small oil-fired boiler should also be given consideration by the smaller grower.

I do know that electric heating will maintain a far more constant temperature and does not require the attention as do boilers, whatever type they may be. I would advise my readers to consult a good electrical engineer on the question of electrically heating their greenhouses.

If carnations are grown in a completely cold greenhouse, very few flowers, if any, will open during winter: many will damp off, although only heavy frost would kill the plants.

If, for financial or other reasons, the above suggestion for heating cannot be adopted, it would be possible to provide some temperature by means of ingenious use of an ordinary fumeless oil heater. There are greenhouse oil heaters on the market which will burn reasonably well for forty-eight hours on one filling of a good paraffin oil. Such a heater would be sufficient to keep frost out of the greenhouse and in many cases would provide a temperature of five or ten degrees above outside conditions.

3. *Temperature*

THERE ARE varying opinions as to how much heat is required to grow carnation plants successfully, but anyone with any experience at all will readily agree that cool-grown stuff is of better quality and has more vigour than the warmer-grown plants. If a moderately high temperature is kept during winter, a larger quantity of bloom is obtained; while if grown cool, the number of blooms per plant is reduced. But again, those we do cut are of more substance and better colour, besides which, plants thus grown maintain their vigour and do not give that sickly appearance during spring, so often noticeable with plants grown in a forcing kind of temperature.

I would definitely say that a winter temperature over 45°F. is detrimental to the well-being of the carnation plant; although not an impossible proposition for a well-experienced grower, who can, by feeding correctly, to some extent prevent the softening of the plant. I would therefore advise the beginner to aim for a temperature of 40–45°F. if possible, especially during prolonged spells of dull weather, when it would be advisable to lower the temperature two degrees or so.

In the south it is not uncommon to over-winter plants in the greenhouse without any artificial heat at all; even if the temperature should drop to 34 or 35°F. I would not worry unduly. During a recent winter, when conditions were mild for the time of the year, we did not light any boilers, with the exception of the propagating house fire and those for houses where the young plants are potted into the first pots. All bloom houses were grown entirely cold, and with the approach of the following spring, it was very noticeable how these plants stood up to the April sunshine without any embarrassment or signs of flagging.

Needless to say, the number of blooms we cut during that winter was below average, but it was also our experience that far less 'seconds' were found in the sorting prior to sending blooms to market, than was usual. At the same time such plants,

14

cool-grown, with ventilation when possible, are more resistant to insect infestation and are not so subject to disease.

The ideal winter temperature then would be about 40°F., and do not hesitate to give ventilation on all suitable occasions, always avoiding draughts.

If suitable heating is installed, one should remember that it is not only used for maintaining a temperature around 40–45°F. Especially during autumn and in particular from late September throughout October and November, a thermostatically controlled heating system might well not come into operation when the outside temperature is such that the thermometer in the greenhouse does not fall below 40 or 45°F., yet it might be advisable to provide some measure of artificial heat to maintain a dry atmosphere. Humidity during that time of the year can be very high, causing condensation on the inside of the greenhouse glass. Such conditions are harmful to carnation plants and blooms. It would be advisable to give adequate ventilation and provide some form of heating to encourage air circulation around the plants. It is a point which I know is so frequently overlooked yet is so important.

4. Beds and Benches

AS I SHALL be dealing with pots and potting later on I will only describe the beds or bench system now. In both cases adequate drainage is essential.

We are frequently asked what we commercial growers mean by 'beds'. I would briefly explain as follows: Timber boards, asbestos strips or similar material some 6in. to 7in. wide are set up on the general ground level of the greenhouse to provide a receptacle or trough which can be filled with compost in which the plants are planted out. Approximately 10in below the top of these sides, a good layer of brick rubble or clinker is placed to give the necessary drainage, leaving at least 7in. depth below the top of the sides to take the soil mixture in which the carnations are grown.

Beds with solid bottoms are also very popular. All our

commercial beds are of the solid bottom type. I prefer to make these bottoms of concrete some 2in. thick and shaped like a shallow 'V' i.e., slightly sloping from the sides to the centre which is some 2in. or 3in. lower than the sides. Place a 2in. land drain, a half round tile or even a length of half round galvanised guttering upside down along the centre of the bed in the lowest part of the V through the entire length of the bed for drainage channel. A gentle fall, approx. 1in. in every 10ft. run of bed should be allowed for when laying the concrete, to give the surplus water a free outlet at the lowest end of the bed.

The line of land drain or guttering should be covered with approx. 1in. layer of ¾in. washed shingle and the drainage will have been taken care of.

We shall presume that the soil in the greenhouse is a good fibrous loam, in which case this can be used to fill the beds. Otherwise a good loam with plenty of fibre has to be brought in. As quite a number of ingredients have to be mixed with the soil, we only fill the beds to within some 2in. from the top.

To every four parts of loam we add one part of well-decayed horse manure. I mention specifically horse manure, but this I would only use if the soil is heavy, while on lighter soils, farmyard or even cow manure would do equally well. On all soils it would be well to incorporate also a little mortar rubble or brick rubble to ensure an open mixture, and finally, a dusting of chalk lime and a good carnation base manure, according to maker's directions. Charcoal is a very good substance where soil is inclined to turn sour quickly.

The beds, thus prepared and well mixed, are ready for raking. Contrary to the old belief in treading the beds to consolidate really well, I would only press the soil along the edges of the beds with the back of the rake while levelling off and preparing for planting.

Admittedly, carnations like a fairly firm soil but after the beds have had two or three waterings they will settle down by the time the plants become established. It should be possible to plant with the fingers, instead of a trowel, making a hole to receive the soilball of the plant as it is knocked out of the pot.

The method of benches, or raised beds, is very similar, the only exception being that these beds are raised above ground level, allowing an air space below. Naturally a base, or bottom, is required, and this can be made with concrete paving slabs, tiles, or part asbestos sheets (full sheets, 8ft. × 4ft. cut in half lengthways).

If a raised bed is made 4ft. wide, it is easy to make a bottom with asbestos sheets, ½in. thick, cut in half lengthways, giving a strip 8ft. long and 2ft. wide. Place a row of bricks on edge the entire length of the proposed centre of the bed, on which one edge of the asbestos will rest, while along the sides of the bed, bricks are placed at intervals of one every 12in. on the flat.

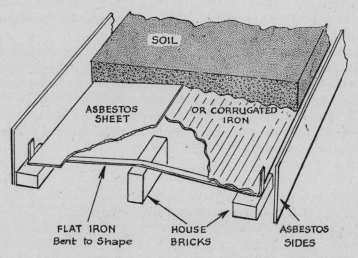

FIG. 3 Section of raised bed

This completed, we have a bottom slanting from the middle to each side. Strips of asbestos 8in. wide and 8ft. long are now placed on top of the base to form the sides and these are held in place by stakes driven into the ground. It is not essential to secure the sides to the stakes as the soil we place in beds will stop them from falling inwards. Ends are placed into position, and the raised bed is ready for filling with soil. The same mixture can be used as already described, but of course it is not necessary to use clinker or brick rubble as a base to provide drainage, as we shall have all the drainage we require in this type of bed.

These beds are very simple to make, yet most effective and certainly lasting. When using asbestos, however, it is best to use ⅜in. thick for the sides and ½in. for bottoms and not the ¼in. which normally is easier to obtain.

Fig. 3 shows you a close-up of a raised bed in one of our houses. Here we have used a concrete paving slab 2ft. × 2in. supported by a metal bar 1½in. wide and shaped to correspond with the brick on edge in the middle and a brick placed flat at each side. To avoid the necessity of using wooden stakes to support the sides, we made the bars longer than required for the base only and bend them upwards 10in., thus making a support for the asbestos strips which form the sides. This is also clearly shown in the Fig. 3.

The advantage of raised beds is in the easier control of moisture during the winter months. These beds also lay warmer than other beds but the disadvantage is felt during a hot summer when they need watering a good deal more. It is with this in mind that a really good fibrous loam should be used. Soil in raised beds should also be firmer, and light treading is often necessary.

5. *Purchase of Plants*

To BEGIN with, the culture of P.F. Carnations is the same as with any other plant, whether it be chrysanthemums, roses, etc. Make sure you buy the right type of stock and that it is clean and sturdy as well as free from disease.

The best growers grow 'stock plants' for the specific purpose of producing cuttings only. It has been proved beyond doubt, that cuttings produced from such plants are far superior to those taken from flowering plants. Obviously when the amateur grower does his own propagation it is not possible to grow special stock plants. He should, however, select the best of the cuttings available referred to in the chapter dealing with Propagation.

Nowadays one is apt to hear a good deal also of 'cultured cuttings' which in fact means that all propagating material has been subject to laboratory tissue tests, which, in almost all cases, is beyond the scope of even the small or medium sized commercial concerns let alone the amateur. It is certainly not necessary and the mention of this modern technique does not need to cause any second thoughts on the part of the amateur in any way. All it implies is that the commercial carnation plant producer has, nowadays, means at his disposal whereby he can examine his stock thoroughly and, more or less, guarantee his cuttings free from any vascular disease.

We have practised this 'culturing' at our Sway nurseries since 1955 and the results have been so encouraging that we consider the time taken and the additional expense involved more than worthwhile.

From such 'cultured' stock only the very best plants are grown on to produce the ultimate multiplication stock from which cuttings and plants are supplied.

Many are the sources of supply and equally as many are the disappointments. It may at first appear costly, but then, that applies to everything we buy if quality goods are what we are looking for. Cheap shoes are easily recognised, while a suit of clothes of the best possible material and cut by expert cutters cannot be expected to be cheap. A cheap article could prove to be the most expensive in the long run, and this is more true than ever where purchases of cheap plants are concerned.

To commence then with the best possible plant, one should only purchase from a well-known firm, preferably from one who specialises in P.F. Carnations, for he, as well as his staff, will be experienced, and not only that, will be most particular about selecting his stock and propagating material—so essential to maintain one's stock at the highest possible level.

Once a good stock is in our possession, we may prefer to propagate our own in the future and only make occasional purchases for the sake of acquiring some new variety we may see at one or another show, and which takes our fancy either for colour, habit, or the many things we like in a plant, but on which we all differ!

For the reason then of maintaining our own stock by means of propagating cuttings, it is of the utmost importance that we start with the right type of plant of a vigorous and healthy stock. It is from this single plant that we shall propagate our future plants and it must be obvious to readers who have followed me so far, that no good can be expected if the results obtained from the parent plant are not all we would have liked them to have been.

6. *Plant Purchase and its Problems*

NOT AN uncommon question is: 'Is it best to buy rooted cuttings or young plants in small pots?' The answer is complicated and needs clarification. The cheapest way would naturally be 'rooted cuttings'. Commercial growers always buy their new plants this way of course, when they pot them and have the necessary facilities to house and look after them until they eventually are planted in the beds or potted on for stock. It calls, however, for some skill and it is only to the more experienced amateur grower that I would recommend this method of purchasing their requirements.

The best way, slightly more expensive but more certain of results, would be to purchase plants in pots, 'stopped and broken'. Let me hasten to explain the meaning of this term, because I recall one occasion when I submitted a quotation to a beginner and emphasised that the plants we would supply were well established and 'stopped and broken' whereupon he replied, rather disgustedly, that he was not prepared to accept broken plants.

It means of course that all plants would have received the 'first stop' and are forming their natural 'breaks'.

Young plants in small pots are normally available from approximately the middle of April and were cuttings propagated during December and January. It will be clear therefore that such plants, although delivered at a later date than rooted cuttings, are virtually the same, in actual fact they should be better for more skilful attention has been given to them by the nurseryman who has better facilities during that tricky part of the year and thereby are able to produce a better plant than is possible by the average amateur.

Briefly, therefore, I would in most cases suggest a preference for young plants in pots, except for those who have handled successfully, rooted cuttings during the period January to March.

The next would be the question: 'Which varieties should we order?' I find it almost impossible to give any ruling on all the colours and shades or colour combinations which are available in carnations. Our tastes for colour vary so widely.

To a beginner I would always suggest a 'collection' consisting of either six or twelve plants in assorted colours and varieties which are selected by the nurseryman according to stock available.

I cannot speak on behalf of all specialists supplying carnation plants, but I would assure anyone, holding the belief that— 'collections' of plants and growers' selection—and offered at a much lower cost than list prices, must obviously be of inferior quality, to be completely misinformed. A good specialist who has a reputation to maintain and is desirous of retaining the confidence which is so necessary in our industry, would not be so foolish as to offer an inferior plant to his customer even at a lower rate. Such a practise would be very short sighted as the horticultural plant trade depends to a very great extent on recommendations. In our own nurseries for instance it often happens that more plants of certain varieties have been propagated than are required or have been ordered at a later date, and it is better to include these in collections than have them on hand until they are of no further use, even if these varieties should be the higher priced ones.

Furthermore, orders for collections can be handled more quickly and consequently are not charged with the same overheads as orders which have to be collected individually before despatch from the various locations on the nursery.

I can say with positive certainty that the amateur never need to have any doubts about ordering a collection as such. There would be such colours as white, pink, scarlet and one or two 'fancies,' which to start with would be a nice assortment. At a later date it may be that one or two other varieties would be preferred which are then ordered individually to augment one's collection.

It will be realised that, when at first we go through one or another carnation specialist's price list, the prices quoted may seem rather expensive; in fact, that is not the case, provided that good strong stock is secured. For a specialist, to maintain a first class stock can be very expensive if he does the job correctly, and makes a real and true effort to maintain a careful selection of plants from which his cuttings are taken.

Compare prices of bedding plants for instance, say a box of bedding plants for your garden; normally eighteen to twenty-four small plants raised from seed, and no more time spent on them than just sowing and pricking out, mostly in unsterilised soil, may cost you from six to eight shillings. But these plants are annuals, and we must therefore buy each year a fresh supply, carnations, however, are different. Once a stock has been bought it is there for as long as we care to propagate from it, so long as we keep that stock healthy and clean. An occasional purchase of a new variety which attracts us, to replace one which has become too old, or which we do not fancy as well, and our interest in the cultivation of the P.F. Carnation will grow as experienced is gained.

Finally, there are plants in 5in. pots which can be purchased. It is, however, the price which causes one to ponder. The first impression may be that these plants are too costly for, on average, they may cost double the price of plants in 2½in. or 3in. pots. It should be remembered, however, that such plants were originally propagated at more or less the same time as those offered in the smaller pots and have had to be looked after, etc., not forgetting the actual potting-on and all it entails. Such plants are usually available from the specialists by mid-August and throughout September, October and November. Therefore the nurseryman has had the care of such plants for something like seven or eight months. Specialist care has ensured that the plants have been stopped correctly and by the time they are despatched they will be either in bud or showing their first blooms. Certainly a very attractive proposition. Finally, and a matter which should also be borne in mind, is that such plants will provide a supply of cuttings during the coming winter months which could be propagated and thus produce the new young plants for the following year. One such plant in a 5in. pot, producing blooms throughout the winter from the time they are received, could, in addition, well produce

1 (a) A carnation bed 4ft. wide, 7in. deep at sides and 10in. deep in centre. Constructed of concrete 2in. thick at sides and 3in. thick at bottom; the whole of the bed having a fall of 1in. in 10ft. Note drain pipe.

1 (b) Concrete bed with centre drain covered with ¾in. shingle to take 7in. depth of soil

2 (a) A typical commercial bed. concrete paths showing short metal flat iron uprights cemented in path to support either wooden or asbestos sides 8in. wide and varying in length

2 (b) Testing cuttings at our laboratory at Sway

four or five new plants by the following February. From the foregoing it is not difficult to see that this may well be the most economic proposition of all.

Whatever one decides upon, I cannot emphasise enough the importance of ensuring that plants purchased are from a firm which specialises in carnations, as, so often, I am sorry to say, plants of inferior origin cause sufficient disappointment to cause the grower to lose interest in the culture of carnations; whereas had he started with plants from a reputable source, which possessed vigour, good health, etc., his interest would have increased and his joys would have grown to an almost unlimited extent.

7. *Cuttings Versus Seeds*

THE USUAL way, in fact the only way, to ensure true reproduction of one's varieties is by means of cuttings. We are often asked for a packet of seeds of this or that variety and no doubt many think this is the way in which P.F. Carnation plants are produced.

Without contradiction, these carnations can be and are originally grown from seeds; at my nursery we grow many thousands of seedlings each year, but these are not for our flower production but solely for the raising of new varieties. Crossings are made each summer in an endeavour to bring out the better qualities of one variety and merge them with another. Almost a complete year has to elapse before we can see if our wisdom (or is it ignorance?) has been correct. By this, I mean that before we can see the result of our predetermined crossing, we have to wait a complete year before the seedling thus obtained will show its first blooms and which, we hope, will be something new, or at least an improvement on what we already grow. It may all seem very interesting and very simple, but I assure you that disappointments are many. One cannot know what results to expect from P.F. Carnation seedlings; in many cases a large percentage of them may be single blooms. By this I mean a small bloom on a very long stem as a rule, with no more than four to six petals—an absolutely useless article.

B

It is clear then that carnations grown from seed are not necessarily reproductions of the actual parent plant. In fact, from one seedpod as many as from forty to sixty seeds may be obtained which, when sown, could easily result in each and every plant thus produced being different in one way or another. Some may be very tall; others dwarf and bushy. It is by careful planning and working to a predetermined sort of pedigree programme, that it is possible to raise some new variety worthy of registration with the British National Carnation Society.

To maintain a stock of a certain particular variety with its own particular habit, character of plant, and colour of bloom, we must propagate from cuttings.

Only by this method can we reproduce a variety possessing the identical characteristics, substance, colour and vigour, although by careless selection of cuttings, vigour especially can easily be lost, but more will be said in a subsequent chapter.

In conclusion, therefore, I would suggest that carnations are grown from seed only after one has established a healthy stock of well known and proved varieties and their culture is well understood and appreciated. Only then would I say that sowing seed could provide an added attraction and interest. From the foregoing and more particularly now, since the standard of present day varieties stands very high, it will give a good deal of disappointment, but it could well be possible to be fortunate enough to find perhaps one which has outstanding merits. After all I can think of one variety of recent years, namely, FRAGRANT ANN, which was a seedling raised by an amateur in Derbyshire and is indeed an outstanding example. I am sure many of my readers have a 'flutter' on the football pools and eagerly check the match results on Saturday, to find again that although the forecast was very near, it was just not good enough. It is the same with trying to raise a new carnation. I think the odds are about equal.

8. *Propagation*

What Cuttings to Take

Vegetative reproduction by propagating side shoots or 'cuttings' reproduces in the main the same characteristics, vigour, etc., as the stem from which the cutting is taken. Needless to say then it is vital to take the utmost care in selecting the plant and indeed the stem from which to take your cuttings.

A well-grown carnation will have a stem varying from 18in. to 36in. in length. Each stem will have approximately twelve nodes or pairs of leaves. Each such node will produce one side shoot which, nearer the top, will be more or less only side buds. These are normally taken off (disbudded), before the main bud attains any size in order to improve the size and form of the ultimate bloom. The very lowest 'breaks' or side shoots are usually very contracted and stubby. These will not be very good cuttings to use as propagating material for they will produce plants which are very slow and usually produce blooms of very inferior quality. Furthermore the plant produced from this type of cutting will be more susceptible to disease.

There is of course a good deal of difference between the methods adopted by commercial growers and those which the amateur will follow. It always will be so and is unavoidable.

The large commercial grower and certainly at our own nurseries, special plants are grown for 'stock'; such plants are from special selected clone stocks and undergo frequent selecting and roguing during the whole season before the propagating period arrives.

All our own cuttings intended to provide the plants for our mother stock department, first of all pass through the laboratory for 'culturing' which implies that each cutting is individually tested for disease within the plant tissue so that we can make absolutely certain that only disease-free material is propagated, which for the entire period of the subsequent two years is grown under conditions of complete isolation. The utmost care is taken to see that there is no likelihood of them

25

becoming infected during the subsequent growing period.

This, of course, is only possible where large quantities are grown and propagated each year. For the amateur grower it is not necessary in any way, provided he maintains a healthy stock and only adds to his collection new varieties and plants obtained from a source of supply which guarantees such plants to be free from vascular disease. In the case of the amateur who normally grows his plants in pots, risk of the spread of disease from one plant to another is lessened, in any case, by the fact that the root system of each plant is confined to the pot in which the plant grows.

It is obvious, too, that an amateur grower could not grow stock plants in the same way as the larger commercial grower, for such stock plants are only allowed to produce one or, at the most, two flowers and all other shoots are 'stopped' throughout the season in order to produce the best type of cuttings. Bearing in mind that the amateur grows all his plants for the flowers they will produce, I would suggest that to compromise, only one, the most vigorous shoot of each plant that one wishes to reproduce, is stopped by the middle of September, or certainly by the end of the month, when four to six good cuttings may be taken during January and February.

Such cuttings when taken are removed with a downward-backward pull in such a manner that the 'heel' or that portion of the base of the shoot which is attached to the main stem is taken off intact.

When a flower stem has been cut back as suggested above, the flower stem which has elongated to form a bud is pinched off at a point above which worthless bud shoots (side buds) are formed. This is usually at the fifth or sixth node below the main bud (see Fig. 10).

If unrooted cuttings are obtained from a commercial plant nursery, it may well be that such cuttings do not show a 'heel' when received. This, however, is no cause for alarm, but is due to a special technique practised by the commercial establishment to save labour, and invariably on a nursery where the use of knives has long been abolished. The reason for this will be explained in a subsequent chapter relating to disease. The fact that such a cutting is broken out instead of pulled off by the 'heel' does not mean that it is a 'top' cutting and therefore undesirable. A top cutting is the tip of a stem which has elongated to form a bud. If the shoot has reached a length of more than 8in. before it is taken as a cutting then it would generally constitute a 'top cutting' and in such a case would seldom make a desirable plant. Such cuttings are distinguished by the length of stem between the nodes and the leaf formation at the tip, and are easily recognised by an experienced grower. Such cuttings would never be sent out by a firm of repute to fulfil orders for rooted cuttings even if supplies were short.

In explaining this aspect, I should add that with such varieties as 'the Sims' which are now very numerous and widely grown, coupled with the fact that due to the many desirable characteristics of Sim varieties, raisers and breeders use these as 'parents' in their breeding programme, and when one remembers that all Sims have a tall habit and consequently tend to pass this on to their offspring, cuttings from such varieties will have more length of stem between nodes than the dwarfer and more compact varieties. This, therefore, should not be confused when cuttings are taken or have been purchased.

Cuttings should be taken only from clean, healthy and vigorous plants. Failure to observe this fundamental rule will cause a variety to deteriorate, will lower production, produce flowers of lesser quality and substance, render the ultimate stock less resistant to disease, and eventually result in a stock which in no way compares with the original.

It should be remembered that most carnation diseases, with the possible exception of rhizoctania stem rot may be carried in the cuttings. Therefore, no plant which shows any signs or any trace or possibility of disease, or which is located close to diseased plants, should be used to provide propagating material.

A danger which occurs too often is that cuttings are taken off the flower stem after they have been cut, either in the nursery grading room or as in the case of the amateur grower when they have been taken into the house, and it is found that a few cuttings are left on the stem. Do not use such cuttings for propagation as it is impossible to know what type of plant they came from or what its environment was and there would always be the danger of propagating from a weak or undesirable plant.

A good deal has often been said about 'over' propagation. This, to say the least, is a misleading and over-rated statement.

It depends on what is implied by over-propagation. Actually there is no such thing, as to my mind, over-propagation is nothing short of careless propagation, and I would interpret this expression to mean; to propagate all and every shoot which can be taken from a plant. It may well be that a fairly bushy plant has no satisfactory cuttings at all and therefore even one top shoot taken from such a plant could be called 'over-propagation', whilst a commercial and well grown stock plant could produce as many as forty or sixty very good cuttings, and if all such cuttings were used for propagation I would consider that 'over-propagation' was the case.

Propagation from diseased or weak stock; taking thin, elongated shoots from the upper part of the stems; taking short squatty shoots from the hard wood at the base of the stem; taking cuttings that are too small, or top cuttings from shoots that have run up to form bud . . . such a practice is careless or over-propagation.

When to Propagate

The propagating season extends from early November until the end of March, although commercial growers, especially those who specialise in offering rooted cuttings and plants for sale often start as early as October and not infrequently propagate throughout the month of April in order to meet the demand for cuttings for very early or late planting. Generally speaking carnation cuttings can be rooted, providing appropriate facilities are available, throughout the twelve months of the year. January, February and March, however, will always be considered to be the most desirable months for propagation of carnation cuttings. This, in particular, I would suggest for the amateur grower.

The slower growing varieties are best propagated early, whilst those varieties which are more rapid would be better left until February or March.

Preparing the Cuttings

The quicker cuttings are 'prepared' and inserted after they have been taken, the better. It would be wrong to leave cuttings to wilt and if for some reason or other cuttings cannot be handled very soon after they have been taken from the plant, it is best to put them in a polythene bag which should be closed at the top and kept in as cool a place as possible.

Properly handled, cuttings can be kept for a fairly long period, and, in fact, this is a practice which is followed on a few of the most up-to-date commercial nurseries. We have experienced, that by means of refrigeration, cuttings can be kept for eight or nine months quite satisfactorily. I should warn the ambitious and experimentally minded amateur, however, that the ordinary domestic 'fridge' will not serve the purpose even if one's wife would spare you a small corner. The temperature in such a small refrigerator will not be maintained accurately enough. The temperature variation for the suitable storage of cuttings is very critical and should not exceed 32°F. or fall below 31°F. Furthermore, the temperature in a domestic appliance varies between the top and the bottom, besides which, the more frequent opening of the door causes fluctuations which will be detrimental to the cuttings.

The type of refrigerator such as we use ourselves varies from 400 to 1,500 cubic feet capacity and has, as well as a refrigeration, a small heating plant installed. The latter comes into operation directly the temperature drops below 31°F. when at the same time the cooling motor is switched off. When the temperature rises to above 31°F. the heater is cut out and when 32°F. is reached the cooling element motor cuts in and so on. In addition to such installation, we have small low volume fans fitted, at least three for a 400 cu. ft. cold box and more or larger fans for the larger cool room, which are essential to maintain not only air movement but also ensure that one part of the refrigerator is not cooler or warmer than the other.

Although I cannot see such refrigeration and storage of cuttings becoming a practice which will be adopted or indeed required by the amateur carnation grower, the above brief explanation might be timely, especially as more and more of such up-to-date methods are brought into use in the commercial field and one is bound to hear more frequently in the future about 'refrigerated', 'cultured', 'heat-treated' cuttings and so on.

As we continue with this chapter I will first of all endeavour to explain the conventional and long practised method, and subsequently will refer to a more modern way of achieving the same result. Wherever practicable I will at the same time give the reasons which caused such a change in what was considered for so long to be the absolutely correct way of doing things.

So let me go on with the preparation of the cuttings. It has for a long time been a wise practice to treat the cuttings before preparation with a fungicide and may be an insecticide, before they are placed in the propagating bin or frame. This may be done immediately they are removed from the plants. It is better to do this before they have been prepared. The treatment consists of immersing the cuttings in a solution containing fungicide and insecticide, which must be chemically compatible, and water added according to manufacturer's directions. I hesitate to prescribe any particular fungicide or insecticide for this purpose; new chemicals are constantly introduced on to the markets and I am sure that whatever I recommend at the time these notes are being written, it will be superseded by new materials five years from now. I will, therefore, confine my suggestion to what is our practice to date in 1961. We use a Zineb base fungicide in combination with T.E.P.P. insecticide. 3¼ozs. Zineb (Murphase wettable), 11 c.c. T.E.P.P. to 10 gallons water. The cuttings are immersed from five to ten minutes, a period more than sufficient to destroy all fungal spores and kill whatever insect pests may be present.

Cuttings should never be placed in clear water before insertion even if by so doing one is apt to think that they become more crisp and therefore would be the better for this drink. Such a practice would be the most certain invitation to the spread of disease from perhaps only one unexpected but disease-infected cutting.

If the cuttings were taken from the plants with the 'heel' intact, a sharp, but clean knife, should be used to make a cut directly below one of the lower nodes. The two leaves immediately above the cut are removed and no further trimming should be done.

The more up-to-date way, however, would be to break the cutting at one of the nodes, where a reasonably clean break can be made. The reason why I mentioned the old method first, is because one of your old gardening friends who in the past has always had great propagating success, might tell you that what I am saying now is all 'rubbish.' 'I have used my way for the last thirty years and sharpen my knife like a razor. The result is that I strike nine out of every ten cuttings I put in.' It is exactly what I used to say myself only a few years ago. But year by year we make progress. Year by year experimental work all over the world brings us greater knowledge, and it is certainly very true that we have progressed more during the last ten years than the fifty or so years that went before them.

I would at all times recommend disposing of the knives altogether, except for the use of cutting raffia or string for tying the plants, or sharpening the pencil to make certain that the name of the variety is clearly written on the label. It has been proved beyond doubt that where spread of disease was rapid, as well as frequent, it was mainly the knife which was the cause. Discontinuation of its use in the preparation of cuttings, picking of the flowers, etc., showed a remarkable and unmistakable improvement.

Once the art of breaking at the joint has been mastered, and I am sure it will present some difficulty at first, it will later be as easy as cutting with a knife (Plate 34). As before, only the two leaves directly above the break should be removed by pulling off, but only if they are likely to interfere with inserting the cuttings into the sand. So after breaking at the node do not take any more leaves off, i.e. make any more 'wounds', if it can be avoided. Remember that any such 'wound' made is another possible source of infection.

It may be that some of my readers, even after patient practice, will still have difficulty in making a proper break, and the only thing then is to go back to the knife. If there should be a possibility of disease, due to the recent loss of a few plants, I would suggest having a small jar of methylated spirits and a lighted candle so that after each cut is made, the knife can be dipped into the spirit and flamed over the candle, which should destroy any disease organism present on the knife blade. If this is a practical proposition I would, of course, have no objection to the use of a knife.

Frequently, I have been asked as to the virtue or otherwise of the use of rooting hormones. I know there are growers who use these regularly and with excellent results, but I do not use hormones for rooting unless absolutely necessary and I cannot root without it. If cuttings do not root, it is not always due to

B*

lack of hormones, it could be lack of bottom temperature, lack of moisture or incorrect propagating media, such as sand which is too fine or sand which contains too much stone and is therefore too open.

There are a few varieties which even with proper facilities are difficult, and, in such cases, I would certainly recommend the use of a powder hormone. Never would I use a hormone liquid and place cuttings prepared for insertion into an inch or so of such solution for one or two hours. As mentioned before it is a definite invitation to the spread of disease and must be avoided. The use of hormone powder is safe. After preparing the cuttings, dip them about ½in. in the powder and shake off any surplus; then they are ready for insertion.

A common cause for failure in rooted cuttings can be traced to cuttings taken whilst the plants themselves are dry at the roots. I suggest, therefore, that the day before it is intended to gather cuttings, all plants are given a thorough watering to overcome any possibility of failure, at least on this score.

The Propagating Bin or Frame

We need some form of propagating 'bin' or 'frame'. This can easily be made up by using a large-size wooden box some 9in. or 10in. deep. The bottom could be taken out completely and re-nailed with spaces between the boards to encourage free drainage. Alternatively, holes 1in. in diameter could be drilled all over the bottom to answer the same purpose. Another way of making a box for propagating is to take out the bottom entirely and replace this by a few battens, on which are placed tiles—this is the best, for these will ensure all the drainage required as well as retaining moisture (see Fig. 4).

At each end of the box two uprights are nailed from one side to the other; lengthways a strong batten is fixed to form a ridge. Pieces of glass are set slanting from the sides to the ridge and the end can be closed off by glass cut at a suitable angle to ensure complete enclosure of the frame.

Somehow or other it is necessary to provide a little bottom heat underneath our propagating bin so as to maintain a constant temperature of 55°F. in the sand with which the bin will be partially filled.

If you have hot-water pipes in your greenhouse this should

solve the difficulty, as the propagating bin can be placed directly
over the pipes and closed in underneath to conserve the warmth.
I have even heard of people maintaining the necessary tempera-

Fig. 4   Propagation bin or frame

ture under a small propagating box by means of an electric
light bulb. But the best method of all would be an electric soil
warmer, if an adequate number of cuttings are to be propagated.
Advertisements in the gardening papers show that a great many
of these heaters are now obtainable, and if in doubt, ask your
local electrical engineer for advice.

The bottom of the bin, whether wood or tiles, is covered with
a thin layer of coarse but clean ashes or broken-up clinker, but
ensure at all times the utmost cleanliness.

If propagating in pans which take approximately twenty-five
to thirty cuttings, the pans, after cuttings have been inserted,

are placed on the ashes; but as I would prefer to propagate direct into the frame, I would fill the bin with some really clean-washed, sharp sand to a depth of 3in. to 4in. Water this sand well and firm it by means of a wooden rammer, i.e. a flat piece of wood with a handle. After firming, water once more and all should be set to commence inserting the cuttings.

There is, however, something to be said for propagating in pans. It is true that cuttings in pans can easily be taken from the frame, prior to potting, for hardening off, and this is an advantage. But more care needs to be paid to the watering for it can easily be overdone. Sand in a bin maintains the moisture longer than sand in shallow pans. One could, however, place the pans on a layer of ashes in the propagating bin, but I will leave these minor details for you to work out to suit your different conditions. Propagating pans are usually some 6in. to 7in. in diameter and from 3in. to 3½in. in depth. They are provided either with a large drainhole, in the centre of the bottom, or three smaller ones at the sides. The hole or holes are covered with a good crock and are then filled with clean-washed sharp sand. Always make certain the sand is perfectly clean. If in doubt, a thorough washing is advised. The pans are filled to within ½in. of the rim and well watered in. After being left to drain from half an hour to one hour, they are ready for insertion of the cuttings.

When it has been decided not to use pans, but to propagate direct into the bin, sand is placed on the ash or clinker covered bottom to a depth 3in. to 4in., which is quite sufficient. This also should receive a thorough watering, and after firming with a piece of flat wood, cuttings may be inserted.

From my experience, I do not think one need firm the sand too much, provided always a sharp sand is used of not too fine a texture. Very fine sand such as preferred by a bricklayer for building purposes would not be suitable.

For those who take the matter really seriously and do not mind some initial expense in order to be up-to-date, I would suggest something of a revolutionary idea in plant propagation. I refer to 'mist-propagation.' The advantages are numerous but the cost may be the deciding factor and might only be warranted for those who propagate a fair number of cuttings, not necessarily carnations only, for a mist propagation unit could be used for almost any type of cutting, all of which will strike more easily; even those species which are considered really difficult will not present the problem they do in the more conventional way. The cost, including a soil warming cable would be in the region of £20. (See Fig. 5.)

This book is not intended as a free advertising media but having had every success with our own mist propagating installation after having tried out at least two of different manufacture, I feel justified in mentioning the appliance we

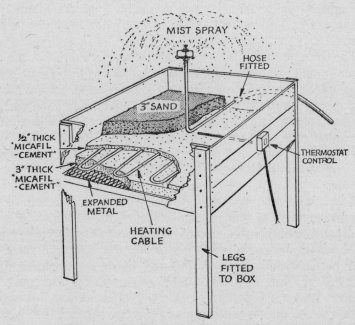

FIG. 5   A single mist-propagation unit

have had in use on our Sway nurseries since 1955. It is supplied by Messrs. MacPenny of Bransgore in Hampshire and has been exhibited at the Chelsea Show as well as at Southport. It is simple but efficient and works equally well for the small unit as it does on the very large scale.

It consists of a 'unit' solenoid valve with filter and an electronic leaf, if the latter is the correct name, for it does not in any way represent a leaf as we know it, but is a small and specially designed control apparatus containing two electrodes which are connected by a film of moisture when placed amongst the cuttings and thus prevents the mist from operating. Directly the moisture film is evaporated the contact between the two electrodes is broken and causes the operation of the solenoid valve which is connected to the ordinary mains supply, and a very fine mist like spray is emitted from the specially designed nozzles.

Each nozzle will cover an area of 5ft. in diameter. It would of course be difficult to make a circular propagating frame for the smallest unit. The best way would be to prepare a suitable frame, say 2ft. square with the one misting nozzle placed in the centre.

The better idea, if sufficient use could be made of the available space, would be a propagating bench, 3ft. wide and 5ft. 6in. long, which would be adequately served by two nozzles, each one being positioned 1ft. 4½in. from each end, leaving a distance of 2ft. 9in. between the nozzles. It should be remembered that the greater part of the cost is in the 'unit' and the 'solenoid valve', the price of each nozzle being only small in comparison. It is well to make the propagating area large enough.

To complete this 'set-up' I would make a special bottom to the bench or frame and incorporate a mains-operated heating cable to dispense with a costly transformer. This bottom must have perfect drainage and is best made by using a mixture of four parts Micafill, obtainable from builders merchants and intended for use as an insulating material, to one part of cement. Water is added and a thorough but not too wet a mix should be the aim. A bottom made of a few laths covered with a thin old sack would be ideal on which to place this mixture. It should be lightly levelled off and not rammed or consolidated. Just levelled off is all that is needed otherwise the porosity of the bottom will be impaired. The first layer should be approximately 3in. thick and will set by the next day.

The heating cable is laid out on this. (I must give a word of warning here and recommend you to consult your local Electricity Board, where free advice can be obtained as to the length of cable required according to the temperature required, also full technical details may be obtained from this source).

The next operation is to place a 1in. layer or rendering of

the foregoing Micafill/cement mixture over the cable. The surface is trowelled backwards and forwards without undue pressure on the trowel so as to give a smooth surface on which afterwards one can use a shovel for removal of sand. This surface will be quite hard and firm and yet will drain as freely as a sieve.

Only 2in. or at the most a depth of 2½in. sand or other propagating media is required.

Thus the temperature as well as watering and hand syringing is taken care of. The latter by the electronic leaf already mentioned, and the bottom temperature by means of a rod-type thermostat which is placed horizontally about ½ in. above the permanent bottom of the bin, and extending from the side for its entire length (usually some 18in.) into the sand.

For ordinary propagation, a temperature of 58–60°F. is required but where the 'mist unit' is in use my recommendation would be a 10° increase. The ambient or air temperature of the house in both cases should not be higher than 52–55°F. Especially under mist, ventilation should be given freely when conditions permit and the overhead air temperature should not be allowed to increase without opening the ventilators.

After two to two-and-half weeks, cuttings under 'mist' will be making roots and mist should be operated by hand. We call this the process of 'weaning,' i.e. the number of 'bursts' of mist are determined and the system is manually operated by means of a switch. It depends, of course, on weather conditions at the time. If the day when 'weaning' is to commence is dull, and 'dew' on the plants is fairly heavy, all that will be required is one or two bursts during mid-day or afternoon. During a sunny day the number of bursts are increased accordingly.

The next day the number is reduced and unless the third day is extremely sunny and warm, no mist will be needed. It is obvious too, that at that time the temperature in the sand can be reduced and the thermostat setting lowered to maintain a steady 60°F.

By the end of the third week or certainly by the beginning of the fourth week the cuttings are ready for potting.

There are some who would prefer to use propagating pans, whilst others would rather propagate direct into the frame. Insertion in this form can be made easier if a piece of flatboard the size of the pan is used, with a handle on the upper part and nails which protrude through the board approximately 1in. are driven through and are spaced so that a 6in. pan accommodates approximately twenty-five cuttings. Press this board into the sand, which has been watered thoroughly, and the position for each cutting will be clearly marked after the nail-board has been withdrawn. The small holes left will prevent damage to the base of the cuttings caused by insertion into the sharp gritty sand.

For cuttings to go directly into the propagating bin, we use a straight edge the width of the frame. Lay this in position where the row of cuttings is to be placed, and along its edge draw a line with a knife, approximately ¾in. or 1in. deep. When cuttings have been inserted some 1in. or 1¼in. apart on this line, place the straight edge alongside the row again and tap firmly with a light hammer. In both cases, pans or direct into bin, cuttings should be lightly watered in, and the bin immediately covered with glass.

Shading may also be necessary during bright spells to avoid unnecessary transpiration by cuttings which cannot replenish their moisture requirements until roots have formed, but over-shading must be avoided. During the first week or ten days it may be necessary to syringe the cuttings with a fine hand syringe to avoid wilting, but this too should not be overdone. Obviously there would be more need of this in prolonged bright weather than during a period of dull and humid conditions.

Watering should be attended to. It is impossible to lay down any definite ruling on this for it depends on how quickly the sand or propagating media will dry out. Keep it reasonably moist at all times and, on average, I would say that once a week the watering can would be needed whilst the frame is closed, but directly ventilation is given the process of drying will be hastened. However, I only mention this as a guide, and observation is necessary in order to determine when or when not to water cuttings.

At the best of times there will be occasions when cuttings do not 'strike' as well, or at all, as we would expect them to, even when everything seems to have been provided to ensure good results.

There are certain varieties which always cause difficulty and we usually refer to them as 'difficult strikers'. As already mentioned earlier, hormone powder will often give better results.

Another cause or reason for bad rooting or total failure would be that cuttings were taken from plants which were too dry at the root. This must always be avoided and if in doubt it is as well to give the plant, to be propagated from, a good watering the day before taking cuttings.

A further word on the propagating media would not be amiss. We have already mentioned sharp sand, I should emphasise this point. Sand can vary a great deal and I have experienced unbelievable disappointments with different deliveries of sand which came from the same pit. Whilst one seam may be perfect for our purpose, the next seam may be totally unsuitable.

I have no doubt that the finest media for propagation is 'Perlite' but I regret to say that this material is not obtainable in this country. It is a volcanic ash and is obtainable from the works in Germany. The cost is not high but the transport cost coupled with import duties, etc., make it prohibitive. The next best thing is 'Brelite', in appearance similar to 'Perlite', except that it is much finer. I would not say that it has many advantages over sand except that it can be relied upon to be the same all the time, so that once one has learned how to use it, one can repeat the usual routine, and this cannot be said for all samples of sand.

Vermiculite is another media which is recommended by some. It is claimed that cuttings will root 'freely' in a shorter space of time. Our experiments found this to be true.

In fourteen days we could take the cuttings from the pans for potting into 2in. pots, and all were rooted far better than a corresponding batch of the same variety, taken at the same time, but inserted in sand. We were very much impressed and were already working out how many more cuttings we would be able to propagate in the given space during the entire propagating season. I kept a very careful check on these two batches throughout all stages, as did our foreman who was even more enthusiastic than myself. Both batches received similar treatment and were eventually planted out after potting in the usual way in a small house which we kept for experimental work of this kind. Everything went well for some time; I think the plants propagated in this special media were slightly ahead for a while. Later there was very little difference in either batch until late summer, when a few plants looked sick and became somewhat stunted. Breaks were few and far between, while the batch raised and grown in our normal way were in first class order and showing a promising winter crop.

Some time later, a few plants had to be removed, for we did not like the look of them at all. Others were now not looking as well as we would have liked, and our anxiety increased each week, especially as we had given some plants from that same batch to a grower friend who was to try them out in his nursery. We received a similar report from him later. The dead plants removed from the bed were thoroughly examined and afterwards burned. It was found that the base of the plant, where as a cutting we had made the basal cut, had enlarged considerably. The lower underground portion was more like a multitude of 'warts' mingled together.

This, of course, made me think. During the actual winter months we had no further losses, but with the approach of the following spring, with prolonged periods of bright sunshine, we lost many more plants from the batch propagated in this 'new' media. By May we had lost the entire lot, while those which originally came from the sand bin were as perfect as ever. They had produced a very good average of blooms and looked just as a good carnation plant should in early spring.

On removing the last few dead plants we again examined them very carefully, and, as with the previous ones, the base was very much enlarged and great cracks were to be found lengthways along the base. My opinion today is that owing to this extraordinarily rapid root formation the plants in the young stage were 'overworked' and although a large and strong action is what we need, I am sure it can be too large.

There was a time that we thought it was infection of Wilt disease, but after plants had been sent away for closer examinations by scientific experts in plant diseases, etc., it was reported to us that no traces of this could be found and no direct cause could be given for the loss of the plants.

The reason for mentioning this experiment, one of many, is to impress upon my readers that, if one can root cuttings quite successfully in a well-tried and long-practised manner, why embark on something new which has not been fully tried out and of which results are by no means certain?

Therefore, use no other material than clean-washed, sharp sand. The temperature of the sand is maintained at approximately 55°F., and shading has to be provided during sunshine, but should be removed each evening or at such a time when it is not serving a useful purpose. Overshading is equally as harmful to the cuttings as no shading at all.

In the second week it will be necessary to see if the pans require watering, but be careful not to water unless really necessary. At no time, however, should the base of the cutting become dry, but at the same time over-watering or watering *ad lib* must be avoided. It is impossible to enlarge further on this question of when to water, as propagations vary so greatly. It also depends, of course, to some extent on the bottom heat as to how soon a frame will dry out sufficiently to require a further watering. This is one of the arts in growing which has to be learned by trial and error.

After the first week a little air could be admitted to the frame by placing a piece of wood under the glass against the ridge, while shading could be dispensed with, except during extremely bright weather. The bottom heat, i.e. the temperature of 50°F. should be our aim. Always keep the overhead temperature from 5–10° below the actual sand temperature.

Fourteen days after insertion the glass could be removed altogether and shading should not be necessary now unless the plants show embarrassment during bright periods. The moisture content of the sand is very important. More ventilation can be given to the greenhouse itself, if weather conditions are favourable, and in the third week we should begin to harden off the cuttings in readiness for removal from the frame for potting up during the fourth week.

As soon as the cuttings are sufficiently rooted, it is important to remove them from the sand without unnecessary delay and to see about potting-up into small pots.

Remember, that while the cuttings are in the sand they cannot find any nutrition on which to sustain new growth, and should they grow at all when still in the sand, this will only be on air and water plus bottom heat, and result in weak growth instead of that sturdiness which we are looking for in young carnation plants.

9. *First Potting*

THE LIFTING of the cuttings from the bin, or pans, should be done with care. With much care and attention we have been able to produce young rootlets on bare cuttings. This has taken us four weeks, or thereabouts, to accomplish, and it would be folly to remove the cuttings in a careless manner so that many of these tender roots are damaged or entirely broken off.

Do not remove too many from the sand at the same time so that they lie about for a considerable time before being placed in the small pot. Should the roots be somewhat dry, dip them in some clean water before potting them into the new soil. Never pot, plant, or re-pot a plant which is dry at the roots.

What Pots to Use

The first type of pots we think of are the conventional clay pots which have been used for many years and there is nothing I can say against them. It is essential, however, that they are perfectly clean if plants have been grown in them before. The best procedure would be to scrub them and if possible to steam sterilize them afterwards. This would make certain that the new plants to be potted could not become affected by any disease which may lie dormant in the pot. The pot should also be dry, for potting into damp or moist pots will later present difficulties when the soilball has to be knocked out for either re-potting or planting.

There are, however, a good many other types of pots which have made their appearance during recent years. There are the mulch paper pots, which I consider unsuitable, and I advise against their use for carnations. They invariably cause nitrogen starvation due to ammonia being absorbed during the decomposition process of the material of which these pots are manufactured, and although the plants at first appear to grow quite happily after some three or four weeks they will become starved and stunted due to lack of nitrogen.

I would not be too happy, either, in using bitumen treated paper pots. They do not decompose as rapidly as one would imagine when they are potted-on or planted out, and consequently the roots become strangled.

More recently polypots, a type of non-porous plastic pot, have been introduced. I think they may have a future for certain types of plants, but at present they are still rather expensive. At the same time we are faced with storage problems and subsequently with washing and sterilizing pots before further use can be made of them.

My preference would be the peat-wood pulp pot, one of which is known as the 'Jiffy' pot. They are now available from almost all garden sundry shops in small and large packs. The cost is reasonable and during their manufacture they are impregnated with plant nutrients whereby deficiencies are eliminated. The plants, and especially carnations, do extremely well in them, and for the first potting I would use the $2\frac{1}{4}$in. size, although smaller as well as larger sizes are available.

About fourteen days after potting it will be noticed that very fine rootlets are penetrating the pot wall and after four or five weeks the whole surface of the pot will be a mass of fine roots. When such plants need to be moved into large pots, 'pot and all' is potted on, but it is essential to make certain that the plants are given a thorough soaking, for if Jiffy pots are potted-on or planted out into beds or borders whilst the pot itself is dry, it will not decompose and the plant will not make headway.

By using this type of pot it is no longer necessary to wash or clean pots and there certainly is no call for sterilizing them which for the amateur as well as the commercial grower is a great advantage.

If it is decided to use clay pots, which would be my next choice, I would use a 2in. diameter pot for the first potting and a soil mixture consisting of a good fibrous loam with sufficient sharp sand or mortar rubble added to form an open mixture. After sifting through a $\frac{1}{4}$in. sieve, a light dusting of chalk lime and a little bonemeal of the finer grade is all that is needed for the first potting soil. No fertilizers, however good, should be added as this may damage the roots which are not accustomed to soil at all, having hitherto been only in sand. We should not aim at this stage at a rapid growth of the plant, but more at the type of healthy root formation on which the plant's future will depend. The latter is more rapid in a slightly hungry soil than in a very fertile soil mixture. The loam used should be sweet and clean. By clean we mean free from pests and disease organism. For this reason, in our nurseries we steam-sterilize all our potting soils. Not only do we get rid of insects which are always present in good turfy loam, especially wireworm and leatherjackets, but we also do away with weed seeds, and thus obtain a really clean soil.

As carnations do not normally take kindly to freshly steamed soil we sterilize well in advance of our requirements. Usually we commence this work about September and do sufficient to last us for a considerable time. We turn the soil after sterilization on several occasions and by the time we actually start preparing the first soils for potting, it has mellowed down nicely.

As an alternative to soil steaming, formaldehyde 1 : 49 may be used, but we cannot expect it to rid the soil of weeds as is the case with steam.

A heap of soil which must have been sifted is heavily watered with the formaldehyde solution and covered over with sacks and a tarpaulin for approximately one week. When the covers are taken off, the heap should be turned at least twice each week for some four weeks. It is best not to contemplate using soil which has been treated with formaldehyde until eight weeks after treatment, and even then we must make certain that no formaldehyde fumes remain in the soil.

Steam-sterilizing always will remain the most certain and efficient way. The larger nurseries have of course a steaming plant, but the average amateur will say at once—'How can I steam a small quantity of soil?' Perhaps you only need a barrow-full for all the potting you have to do. Well, there are several ways and means to overcome your difficulty. There are several types of small sterilizers on the market. One, an electric gadget, claimed to be very efficient, would, in my opinion, suit an amateur carnation grower with a collection of say 100 to 200 plants very well. The cost of this little machine may be more than one is prepared to invest for a hobby, but there are specially prepared carnation soils on the market, prepared ready for use, steam-sterilized in three grades. No. 1 for the first potting of newly rooted cuttings; No. 2 for potting-on into 2½in. pots; and the final potting soil, No. 3 for the final potting-on into 6in. or 7in. pots.

This grade could also be used satisfactorily for filling beds for planting out into final quarters.

Nothing should be added to any of these soils at all, as this would upset the correct balance of ingredients so carefully worked out to suit all the requirements of the carnation plant.

These soil mixtures are the same as we use for our own potting, and we have used them for quite a number of years with proven success. It is regularly tested for its lime content, and the loam used is from some very old meadow or pasture land which is full of fibre.

Needless to say, it would be unwise to use the No. 3 mixture for the potting-on of cuttings just taken from sand. The same would apply if we used the No. 1 mixture for the final 6in. or 7in. potting. Each mixture is prepared for each particular move and stage of growth.

I have already been asked: 'Could I not use No. 1 soil with the addition of some fertiliser for the final potting?' My answer is definitely, 'No.' The texture of the first soil would be too fine for a pot larger than 2in. diameter, and consequently form a lump of soil resembling a block of cement. The No. 3 soil, for instance, is not sifted at all, but is shredded, leaving a much coarser texture.

The next thing is to see that the pots to be used are perfectly clean and dry. They certainly must be dry and should have been brought into the greenhouse sometime beforehand. A wet pot used at potting time will give a lot of trouble later on.

All potting of carnation plants should be done moderately firm. Care must be taken that at each removal, or potting-on, at no time is the plant placed deeper than it was originally in the sand for propagating. Deep potting will often lead to serious trouble and may in some cases even be fatal.

Soil for potting should not be too dry, but sufficiently moist so that when a handful of soil is squeezed together it will adhere in that shape, but when disturbed it will easily crumble.

Actually, potting is simple. It goes without saying that a potting bench should have been prepared with a supply of clean pots and soil beforehand. When attempting potting for the first time, learn to do the job correctly from the very start. It may seem awkward at first, but it will soon become a routine which can be done with closed eyes. Practice makes perfect.

Handle the cuttings with the left hand, and the pots and soil with the right. Thus, with the right hand, scoop the little pot half full with soil and place on the bench in front of you, while with the left you will have already taken a cutting which is then held above the pot with the roots just in the pot. With the right hand scoop up a handful of soil and fill in around the stem of the plant. Taking care not to insert the plant too deep, gently press with the thumb and first finger of each hand the soil around the cutting and tap the pot once or twice sharply on the bench. This is all there is to be done, and the plant is potted. A little more practice and it will be an easy task.

As each plant is potted, place it in a shallow box or tray so that it will not be necessary to walk about each time to set plants down one at a time, but a whole batch will be taken together, or at least as many as your tray will hold. Place the plants neatly in rows on an ash-covered bench and water-in when your day's potting is completed.

The first watering should be done well, so that the entire 'soilball' is completely moistened. The surplus water will drain away, therefore do water generously. Shading needs to be given if the weather is bright, and unless the weather outside is really warm, keep the house closed for the first three or four days. The plants will soon become established and shading could then be omitted, while a little air on the lee-side of the house would be permissible. This is increased as time goes on when, after a week or two, the ventilators can be used quite freely. The temperature after the first three or four days should be approximately 45–50°F. at night. It would be unwise to force growth by maintaining a higher temperature; the plant would soon lose all its sturdiness and become weak and spindly.

After a fortnight 40–49°F. at night is all that is needed. From now on, grow your plants as hardy as possible, within reason of course, but certainly do not coddle them at any time.

Successive watering will be necessary, but great attention must be paid to this, as on no account must water be applied when it is not really needed by the plant, or when the soil is sufficiently moist.

Watering is one of the most difficult matters on which to give advice at the best of times, and it is certainly much more difficult, if not impossible to do so on paper. More is said on this point under the heading 'Watering,' but I would just mention that we must never practise as did the 'Old Lady' with her treasured 'Aspidistra'; every morning a little drop before getting the breakfast, in case she forgot it. This is absolutely wrong with a carnation plant. Continuous watering, when there is sufficient moisture in the soil, would tend to foul the soil and make it sour.

By an occasional drying out, we let air between the soil particles where water was previously, and thus the soil is kept aerated and maintains the right sweetness so much loved by carnation plants.

For some days after potting, the soil in the small pots will not dry out as rapidly as it will do later when the soilball is well filled with roots—then watering may have to be done quite freely. As soon as the ball is well covered with roots it will be time for potting-on into $3\frac{1}{2}$in. pots.

Leaving the plants in the small pots when they are thoroughly rooted through will lead to an over-abundance of roots in such a confined space as a 2in. pot, and we would then say that the plant is becoming 'potbound.' This should at all times be avoided as it spoils plants and results in hard growth and later, insufficient breaks. Prepare everything for the second potting well in advance, and the day before actually doing this work, water thoroughly the plants to be potted.

10. *Final Potting*

AGAIN, clean dry pots are essential, as well as the correct soil mixture. As a larger pot is used, this second potting soil is sifted through a coarser sieve, a $\frac{1}{2}$in. square mesh would be ideal for this purpose. As the young plants will have a nice healthy root system by now, they will begin to search for more nutrition and a slightly enriched soil has to be prepared to build up a strong and vigorous plant.

The main ingredients are again a nice fibrous loam; to every six parts of this, after it has been sifted, we add one part of well-decayed horse manure which is also sifted. Also, some burnt earth, mortar or brick rubble, should be added. Sharp sand is also a good ingredient if the loam is of a heavy type for this will ensure an open soil. A sprinkle of chalk lime, and a good carnation base manure completes the mixture.

As for the first potting the soil mixture must be moist but not too wet.

The practice has always been to pot rooted cuttings first into small pots as mentioned in the previous chapter. The next move was into the 3½in. pot and finally into 6in. or 7in. pots which were the 'finals'. It was considered essential to move the plants in stages from one pot to a larger size. This practice is still reasonably sound although for the more experienced grower not the best.

During the years since 1950 commercial growers have been forced to study the economic management of their nurseries more carefully. The rising cost of labour and other overheads forced them to investigate what was necessary and what could be dispensed with.

In regard to potting, on our nursery many experiments were made in order to see where labour and other costs of production could be saved, and small scale experiments were at first made with potting rooted cuttings direct into final or 6in. pots, as well as planting out in their permanent beds where the plants were to flower. There were, of course, disadvantages such as heating a large commercial house for a comparatively small number of small plants in beds or in 6in. pots. It caused difficulties with watering as well, for it obviously took some time before such small plants made enough root to occupy such a large volume of soil. Watering had to be done very carefully and whether in the greenhouse border, bed or final pot, frequently the plant had to be "ball-watered" only, to maintain moisture around the roots without unduly moistening the entire soil. Soil not occupied by plant roots would become 'sour' if watered continually and after a time would be unsuitable for plant growth.

This method, therefore, called for a good deal of experience, but if it can be managed well it is certainly worthwhile. There is no further check to the plant by repeated re-potting. Once the plant is established it should not experience any further setback and consequently after the plant has been given its first 'stop' a larger number of breaks will be obtained than from those plants which have been given the various moves from one pot to another. I must mention again, however, that it calls for a good deal of common sense.

A somewhat easier procedure would be to pot the rooted cuttings first into the 2in. clay or 2¾in. Jiffy pot, and when rooted through well, to move them into the 6in. or 7in. pot, so dispensing with the intermediate 3½in. pot.

Whether this latter, or the previous method is adopted, great care is necessary with watering. It must be borne in mind that the smaller the plant the less transpiration of moisture takes place and consequently less water is absorbed by the roots. Furthermore, young plants will not be encouraged to produce new roots in an over-moist soil.

For the less experienced, I will go over the stages of potting as we have practised for many generations and which produce satisfactory results. I will leave the more experienced to draw their own conclusions as to which method appeals to them most.

Cuttings inserted in the sand as unrooted cuttings by the middle of January will be potted into the 2in. pots, and the end of February should be approximately the time for potting-on into 3½in. pots. By knocking a few plants out of the pots it will be seen, by the amount of fibrous roots around the soil-ball, if potting-on is necessary.

Everything, such as potting bench, pots, etc., should be ready, as well as a suitable place on which to stand the pots afterwards. The plants themselves should be thoroughly watered at least an hour or so before potting, so that the entire ball is well moist.

Partly fill the 3½in. pot with soil so that when the 2in. soil-ball is placed in the pot the surface is level with the rim of the 3½in. pot. Hold the plant with the left hand and fill in with new soil with the right. The thumb of each hand holding the pot, is placed at the side of the plant, then without exerting any direct pressure onto the soil, the pot is tapped smartly on the bench to firm the soil around the ball. Perhaps a little more soil will be needed in the pot, and that's all. Do not fill the pot too full however, and see to it that the old 2in. ball is not covered more than is unavoidable.

There is no more in potting than just this, and I really cannot understand why some people just cannot do it efficiently after having tried it for a reasonable time.

Place the pots again on an ash- or shingle-covered bench, and water well in. The plants will not require any further attention until they become sufficiently dry to warrant a further watering. No shading will be necessary this time, and ventilation should be given quite freely.

The final potting into 6in. or 7in. pots is done before the roots become too excessive in the $3\frac{1}{2}$in. pots, as this again would lead to undue hardening of the plants, with the consequent result that very few breaks are obtained after 'stopping' and such plants would therefore be useless, or at any rate inferior samples. When nicely covered with roots all over the $3\frac{1}{2}$in. soilball, they should be potted-on into the final pots.

These being pots in which the plants will flower and remain in until the following year, it is natural that the soil mixture should contain sufficient fertility to last quite some time.

Only the best possible loam with a good percentage of fibre should be used. A good horticultural peat, well-decayed farmyard manure (horse-manure for a special heavy loam), sharp sand, brick or mortar rubble form the main ingredients.

As loam samples vary so much it is not possible to lay down any hard and fast recipe. The heavy loam would require more opening material such as brick or mortar rubble, sharp sand, etc., whilst the sandy loam would only need a small amount of these items. Soil lacking in natural humus would be greatly improved by an increased rate of peat and manure, so the following suggestion is intended for an average loam, and the reader should use his discretion and make variations accordingly.

Final Potting Soil

7 parts fibrous loam
1 part decayed farmyard manure
3 parts good horticultural peat

1 part sharp sand

1 part brick/mortar rubble

The whole should be mixed well and to this should be added ¼lb. J.I. Base manure and ¾oz. Chalk Lime per bushel.

Some years ago it was considered that peat was detrimental to carnation culture. It was said that peat made soil sour or lowered its pH i.e. increased soil acidity.

It is strange how from time to time we change our view, but then, I suppose that is progress.

The John Innes Institute concluded experiments on the most suitable soil mixture to suit most plants. They recommended:

John Innes No. 1 mixture for seed sowings

John Innes No. 2 for first potting

John Innes No. 3 for final potting or bed compost.

We ourselves used this formula for some years, and according to our experiments made slight variations and added certain ingredients which suited our purpose, resulting in the above recommendations.

It may be seen that the John Innes Institute recommended a fairly high percentage of peat in their soil mixtures and since then peat has become an accepted and very necessary ingredient. It helps to make heavy or clay types of loam more open and gives to such soils more aeration, whilst on the sandy loam it improves body and adds humus which is usually lacking in such soil.

A small amount of charcoal added to any soil mixture for carnation culture is often an advantage. It is not quite known what role it plays in the soil, but it is believed that it is a soil purifier and absorbs harmful gasses, but this is not very clear. However, we make a regular practice of using it (approx. one 5in. pot per bushel), and as our plants always do extremely well, producing a heavy crop of good quality blooms carried on strong stiff stems, we would not depart from our standard soil mixtures which always contain this measure of charcoal.

Next we get the potting bench ready, with the quantity of final pots required, a fair supply of clean crocks, i.e. pieces of broken pots for covering the drainage hole in the pot, and a rammer, which is easily made from a piece of broom handle some 9in. to 10in. long. Now we are all set for potting.

All plants, have, of course, had a thorough watering before-

hand, and have had time to drain through. Place the pot
before you and place a crock over the hole so as to form a
bridge so that the surplus water may freely drain away. There
is a right way and a wrong way of placing this crock in position.
Often I have seen it put upside down so that it covered the hole
all right but did not encourage drainage, for it almost closed
the hole completely. Now partly fill the pot with the coarser
parts of the soil, approximately half full, so that when we place
the 3½in. soilball in the pot the top of this ball comes level with
the rim of the pot. Before doing so, however, we use the rammer
to firm the soil we have put into the pot, and when we put more
new soil around the old ball this is also rammed, but care must
be taken not to disturb the 3½in. ball as this would cause
breakage of roots, and I prefer to leave the ball intact.

Should, for some reason or other, the plants have stood too
long in the 3½in. pot so that they have become a little potbound, then I would permit the base of the ball to be broken,
but on no other occasion should this be done. However, if
carnation plants have been attended to properly, and if they

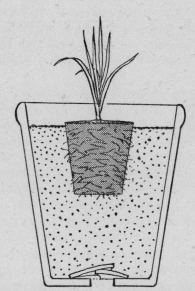

Fig. 6   A plant ex 3in. pot—potted on into 6in. pot. Note: position
of old soilball, also placing of crocks to ensure drainage

have been grown correctly, they should never have become potbound and therefore there should never by any need for this treatment.

When the potting of the plant is completed, the surface of the soil should come to within ½in. or ¾in. from the top of the pot and the old ball should be just visible. (See Fig. 6.) If we were to fill the pot with soil up to the top of the rim there would, of course, be no room for water, and it would be most difficult to moisten the soil if the ball became a little dry.

Obviously, after potting, all plants will have to be watered-in. Do this so that the whole soil content of each pot is moistened thoroughly.

11. *Planting out in Beds*

THIS can be done either from the 2in. pots or the 3½in. size, but I advise you to leave it until the plants are well established in the latter pot. They will by then have had the first 'stop' and should have formed a nice set of 'breaks' or side shoots.

As we have already dealt fully with the making and preparation of the soil for beds or raised benches, we can go straight ahead with the actual planting.

As with potting, see that the plants receive a good watering well in advance. The soil in the beds should be slightly moist, as explained for potting soils, but it should only be slightly firmed, as I would prefer to do all planting by hand and not use a trowel as was our practice years ago when all beds used to be trodden down.

The next step is to mark the bed out, which is not absolutely necessary in the case of small areas, but the longer beds sometimes cause a bit of thought. There are many ways of doing this, and all I would say is: never overcrowd your beds, but give each plant sufficient room for its proper development.

The ideal spacing is 8in. × 9in. The rows across the bed are spaced 9in. apart, while the plants in the actual rows are at 8in. distance from each other. On the other hand, planting 9in. × 9in. is quite all right, and with some varieties which produce plenty of growth and foliage, this would be better. The bushier the plant the wider the spacing should be. Therefore when planting varieties, of which the habit is not known, it is always best to give them that extra space and plant at 9in. each way.

For marking out a bed quickly we use a kind of rake, (homemade), with teeth 9in. apart, with which we rake lines across the bed commencing at the top. Now, if we have a planting stick the width of the bed, with notches cut out at places where

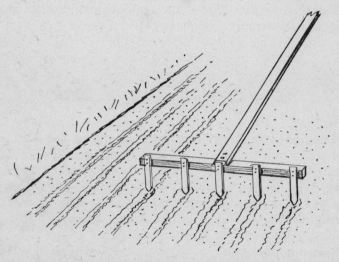

FIG. 7   A marking rake (home made) for quickly and accurately marking out rows when planting in beds

the plants are to go in each row, it will be a very simple matter to keep the rows perfectly straight. (See Fig. 7.)

Make a hole with the hand just deep enough to take a 3½in. soilball, which is placed in position with the surface of the ball level with the surface of the bed; soil is worked around this ball and the whole is pressed firm. A little loose soil may be left over the ball to cover it slightly and so avoid rapid drying out.

If the plants were watered well beforehand, and the soil in the bed was as moist as planting, or potting soil should be, watering-in will not be necessary immediately, except during

3 (a) Various types of cuttings
(from left to right)
1 Taken from the lower part
of the flower stem, should not
be used for propagation
2 The ideal cutting—about
6in. to 8in. in length
3 Another good cutting, slightly more compact
4 Like No. 1 taken from too
low down, contracted nodes,
not suitable for propagation
5 A 'top' cutting, i.e. the top
part of a shoot which has
elongated already too far

3 (b) A cutting complete with 'heel'
showing where to break or cut; the
two lower leaves removed

4 (a) A propagating bin with a mist propagation
nozzle' giving coverage of about 3ft. diameter

4 (b) A 6in. diameter seed pan with about 25 cuttings
ready to be placed in the propagating frame

5 (a) Part of an up-to-date commercial propagating house. Soil warming cables provide a thermostatically controlled bottom temperature, whilst air ducting placed under the benches give the required ambient temperature which is also controlled by thermostat. Mist propagating lines are positioned about 3ft. above the benches

5 (b) An ideal cutting rooted well all round its base

6 (a) Steaming grid in position, to be covered with some 12in. of soil from the next section leaving an open trench the width of the bed and some 7ft. long into which the grid is pulled back

6 (b) A section under steam. When a temperature of 212°F has been reached this should be maintained for 20 minutes

bright, warm weather when a light damping down may be advisable.

Watering-in could be left for a couple of days, but this can be determined by examining the ball which should not have become too dry.

I recommend that the soilball is examined occasionally and less notice be taken of the surrounding soil. It may well be necessary, some couple of days after planting, to water each soilball in a similar manner to that of a small pot about to be watered. A hosepipe with a short length of ¼in. pipe would be ideal, as the direction of the water can be more easily controlled. Only sufficient water need be given to maintain the soilball nicely moist.

This process needs to be repeated each time the ball shows signs of drying out. Depending on weather conditions, it may well be that this must be the method of watering for two, or even three weeks, until the roots are beginning to get a hold in the new surrounding soil.

Then it will be time for a general watering to moisten the entire soil contents of the bed. I would like to see that for this purpose a rose is attached to the end of the hose so that soil washing is avoided.

Some two hours after watering it would be as well to test the soil in order to see if the water has penetrated deep enough. It is only in this way that in the end one becomes more familiar as to the amount of water that is required for future watering which could vary on different types and textures of soils.

12. *Watering*

WE COME now to the most difficult subject, and I wish I could delete this chapter altogether, but I am afraid I would receive so many enquiries on the matter that I will endeavour to enlighten my readers as far as possible as to what is required in this way.

It is impossible to lay down any hard and fast rule on when and how to water. It depends on many things, such as soil used,

C

weather condition at the time, stage of plant, etc. It is more or less a matter of trying to understand the actual requirements of the plant, and to attain this, careful observation must be kept. This should not prove too difficult a matter for an interested grower.

Testing plants in larger pots for moisture is best done by tapping the side of the pot with the knuckle of the finger, a

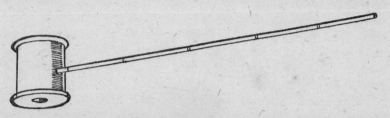

FIG. 8 A simple but efficient instrument made from an empty cotton reel attached to a cane for testing pots for moisture

walking stick, or a piece of cane with an empty cotton reel secured to the end, or any similar home-made device, (Fig. 8), a clear ringing note denotes dryness, whereas a dull noise which sounds solid means that there is sufficient water present in the soil and no watering should be done.

Plants in beds or permanent borders can be examined by pushing a clean, dry cane to a depth of 8in. or 9in. into the soil; if this comes out dirty, and with soil particles adhering, there is no immediate need for water, but should the cane, on removal, be as clean as it was before it was pushed into the soil, then it is time watering took place.

We could also test the beds in various places with the aid of a long but narrow trowel, but care must be taken, so that as little damage as possible is done to the roots.

We ourselves experienced a good deal of trouble by the careless use of the trowel used for such a purpose, and have discontinued this practice. An ingenious idea was put to the test and proved very successful indeed. An odd length of ½in. or ¾in. brass curtain rod, approximately 12in. or 14in. in length was used to make the implement as shown in sketch (Fig. 9). By simply pushing it into the soil to a depth of 9in. or 12in. and giving a full turn, it can be pulled upwards when in

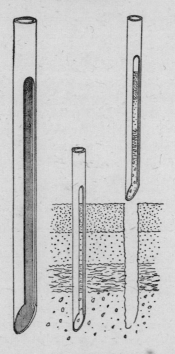

Fig. 9 An easily made soil auger. *Left:* The auger made from
a ½in. or ¾in. brass rod. *centre:* The auger inserted into the soil to a
depth of 9in. or 10in. *right:* The auger withdrawn showing clearly
the soil condition at varying depth

the cut-out portion the condition of the soil at varying depths
can be quickly seen.

The natural growing period of the carnation plant is during
spring and summer, and it is therefore natural that during this
period more water is taken up by the plants. During spells of
hot and sunny weather the plants will evaporate more moisture,
which is taken up from the soil, and consequently the reserve
moisture held by the soil will soon become exhausted if it
is not replenished.

In our nurseries, for instance, it is sometimes necessary to
water the beds in our houses, where carnations are grown for
cut-blooms, twice a week if the weather is bright and warm,
while at other times of the year, when dull and showery weather

predominates, they will go for fourteen days or more without any watering at all.

But I will say this: when we do water, we do it well, and this is a point all beginner carnation growers ought to remember. As an instance: on our nurseries, where our houses are 120ft. long, we have five beds per house, all 4ft. wide. The whole house takes approximately 4,000 plants, and on each occasion when such a house is watered we use 1,000 gallons of water which, if you work it out, is two pints per plant. I would not say that the quantity of water is measured out as exactly as this, but it is the approximate quantity for one good watering, sometimes it may be a little less, other times a little more.

After some experience, and by careful observations, the foliage of the plants will tell you a good deal as to the necessity of watering. Carnation foliage should feel crisp and brittle, but when the leaves feel 'leathery' it may be that they require a watering. First, however, the soil should be inspected, as it could also be due to other causes. For instance, in the spring, after the houses have been a little too warm during the preceding winter, the plants may become embarrassed on the first real sunny day and become limp, but an inspection of the soil may show that this is nicely moist. Thus, here again many points have to be considered.

However, the foregoing is a good guide. I could enlarge on this point by saying that a carnation leaf should snap when bent double between the fingers, but when it folds over like a piece of paper it is almost certain that the plants are dry at the roots, unless a more serious trouble has affected the plant.

Study your plants carefully and I am sure it will not be so difficult nor very long before you will understand the problem of when and how to water.

13. *Stopping*

First Stopping

BY STOPPING we mean the removal of the growing tip of the shoot, or shoots as in the case of the 'second stop'. I will first deal with the 'first stopping', given to plants either in the 2in. or the 3½in. pots.

Some time after potting it will be seen that the plant has got 'hold' of the soil and is beginning to form new growth. Keep the temperature steady and certainly do not encourage—by high temperatures, artificial feeding or over-watering—too quick a growth of the plants. This would produce succulent and sappy growth while it should be our aim to produce sturdy and vigorous plants, which can only be done by steady conditions, free ventilation, and a pleasant atmosphere.

Never 'stop' directly before or after potting; try and work this at least a fortnight before or after each removal. A young cutting potted into a 2in. pot, with a single stem, will grow up and without stopping, will run to flower quickly, producing one single bloom, usually of inferior quality and on a short stem. We have to promote a 'Perpetual-Flowering' plant and for this reason we remove the growing tip of this single stem plant, leaving from four to seven nodes, or sets of leaves, to induce the formation of 'breaks', normally one from each node. Thus a healthy, well-grown plant which after stopping has been left with seven nodes, should produce seven side shoots, forming an ideal and bushy carnation plant, producing, if left unstopped for the second time, at least seven blooms, on good stems and of good quality. But a carnation plant can do even better than that, as will be explained when dealing with the 'second stopping'.

At first it may be difficult, but I am sure that with a little practise, nothing will be easier than to break out nice and clean the top of the shoot to be stopped. Hold the plant by the node, where it is intended to make the break, and with the other hand break the top of the plant sideways. Later it will be just as easy to do this operation with one hand only.

Plants propagated December to January may, during February when still in the 2in. pots, need stopping, but remember, not immediately before they are to be potted-on into 3½in. pots. Usually when the young plant is some 9in. to 10in. tall, one could do this first stopping.

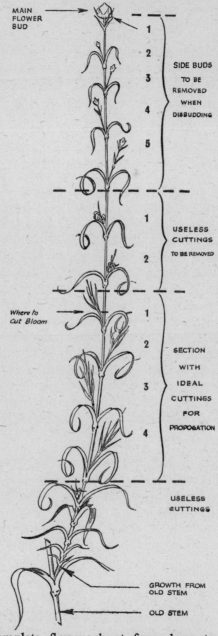

MAIN
FLOWER
BUD

1

2

3

4

5

SIDE BUDS
TO BE
REMOVED
WHEN
DISBUDDING

1

2

USELESS
CUTTINGS
TO BE REMOVED

Where to
Cut Bloom

1

2

3

4

SECTION
WITH
IDEAL
CUTTINGS
FOR
PROPOGATION

USELESS
CUTTINGS

GROWTH FROM
OLD STEM

OLD STEM

FIG. 10 A complete flower shoot from base to terminal bud

Second Stopping

Now the second stopping. This is normally done when the plants are getting established in the final pots, or in the permanent borders.

Some of the breaks resulting from the first stop will have grown away faster than others, and these we call 'leaders'. They are given the second stop first. Never at any time stop all shoots on a plant at the same time. Go over the plants once or twice each week and stop only one or two shoots, when ready.

Removing the tip of all shoots on any one plant would cause a severe and sudden check, besides, they would all form breaks at once, which ultimately would bring along a crop of blooms which flower all within a certain period, while later again, we would have to wait for a further lot of breaks to supply the next batch of blooms. No, our aim should be to produce a constant supply of blooms and for this, as well as other reasons, we must do this second stop in stages as mentioned above.

Again, as with first stopping, we break clean at a node and aim at leaving from five to six joints from which further breaks will come. When speaking of the first stopping, I suggested a plant with seven 'breaks' as a result of stopping. Say we stop only five of the leading shoots for the second stop, leaving two unstopped—usually the lower ones which do not grow as quickly—to run to flower. If each of the five shoots stopped for the second time produced four breaks, this would give us twenty breaks and two flower stems unstopped. So with early propagation, to give the plants an early start in the season, one could in this way produce some twenty-two blooms during the year. I must say, however, that this would not be the case with all varieties. During the many years that I have grown carnations I have learned not to 'count my chickens before they are hatched', and this advice I would offer to all my readers.

I recently heard from a grower friend of mine who stated that a new seedling he had raised, produced the first year, thirty-one blooms per plant. It may be true but it seems a tall story to me; I would certainly like to try out a bed of 1,000 plants and see if the average works out as good.

No second stopping should be done after the end of July,

and should the plants have become quite bushy after stopping only two or three of the leaders, it will not be necessary to go on stopping up to that time.

Plants thus stopped will produce their first blooms some time during September and continue flowering right through the winter. If kept in good health and vigour they should produce blooms for several years continuously, until the plants become either too large to handle, or die of 'old age'.

Commercial growers, however, do not grow their plants for longer than two years; although some of them may keep them for a three-year period, however, these have to be really good plants and not too tall for normal and economic working.

There is a tendency nowadays, for commercial cut flower nurseries to plant very much closer and grow the crop for only one year—planting as close as 3in. × 3in. and only 'one stop'. This would not be a practice I would suggest to the amateur; even for a commercial holding of average size, I would not at the moment consider it of real value, or a proposition which is to be recommended.

I consider that the amateur would get most out of his greenhouse by growing his plants for a two year period. Longer than this would be wrought with difficulties as the plants would become too tall and the quality of the blooms would not be encouraging.

14. *Supporting Pot Plants*

WE SHOULD now consider the best and easiest way to provide the necessary support for the plants grown in pots. The old way of doing this was to place a cane to each plant and tie every shoot with raffia at varying heights. Often the raffia would slip, come undone, or another tie was necessary at almost the same place. The result was an inadequate support for the plants, and an unsightly mess of bunches of raffia.

We now use our special support for all our pot plants; namely the two-legged supports (Fig. 11) for the initial stage before a cane really needs to be used. A 2ft. 6in. or 3ft. cane alongside each small plant some 6in. or 7in. high would look

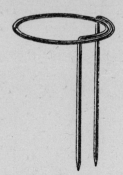

FIG. 11 Two-legged support with 3½in. diam. circle and 'legs'
10in. long

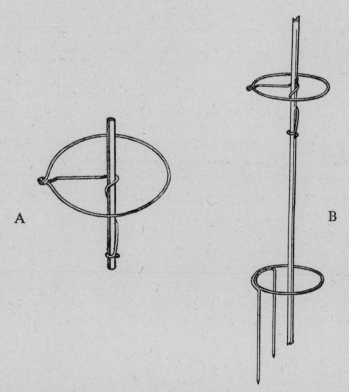

A   B

FIG. 12a and 12b **Cane** ring easily attached to cane or rod.
6in. diam., can be adjusted for height according to needs

C*

quite out of place; and by means of our special support, made of special spring steel wire, the use of canes can be left until a much later date, while the use of raffia has been dispensed with for good. Any shoots growing outside this support's circle can at any time easily be tucked in, and the plants are kept quite tidy and neat. When it becomes necessary to have another support a little higher than the first, we make use of a thin cane, or better still, a thin galvanised steel stake especially supplied for this purpose. The latter, of course, is much neater and does not in the least distract from the beauty of the young plants. Besides, they last indefinitely as against a cane which lasts no more than two or three years at the best.

Still, whether canes or steel rods are used, it is all the same. One is placed to each plant, which is by now in the final pot, and pushed into the soil so that it just misses the original 3½in. soilball, i.e. some 2in. away from the base of the plant. On to this cane, or rod, is clipped our special cane-ring support (Fig. 12 (a) and (b), which has a circle of approximately 6in. or 7in. in diameter, and embraces the entire plant. Another advantage of this support is that one can open its circle to bring within it any shoot which has found its way outside. It can be fixed at any height where it is serving the most advantageous support, and it can be raised or lowered at will. Thus one support is placed above the other as required and a neater and more effective arrangement could not be imagined.

15. *Supporting Plants in Beds*

FOR PLANTS in beds or borders, the two-legged support is used in the same way as for pots. The next support, however, is different. At each corner of the bed an upright post is placed, firmly fixed into the ground and reaching some 4ft. 6in. to 5ft. above the ground. Crossbars are fixed from the left-hand to the right-hand post at 5in. intervals. The same is done at the other end of the bed, while all along the bed at 8ft. to 10ft. distance a similar rack is placed, but of much lighter material, to carry the wires which are later run out between the plants the full length of the bed. (Plate 9b.)

We use a galvanised wire of not too heavy a gauge for the centre wires, but the outside wires need to be a little more substantial as these have to be pulled as taut as possible. The wires are fastened at the one end of the bed, the first layer of wires some 9in. from bed level, and pulled at the other end where they are fastened to the corresponding crossbar. Now the wires are tied down to the intermediate racks and all is set for 'stringing'.

Use a fine cotton twine, and if the beds are the same width at any given point along its length, it is a simple matter to cut a quantity of lengths off beforehand. Use a flat piece of board the length of just half the bed, plus approximately 2in., wind the string from the ball on to this piece of board and cut along the top so as to obtain a bundle of strings all the same length.

Fasten the string to the one outside wire and stretch across the beds along each row of plants, twisting it round each thin wire as you work across the bed, and fasten on to the other outside wire. It would be very much easier if this work could be done by two persons, one on each side of the bed, and each one reaching half way.

In between each two rows of plants we have two strings, thus forming small squares with a plant in each one. After reading all this one may wonder and ask if this is worth the trouble. It may seem an endless job, but really it is not so much trouble, or nearly as complicated as it appears in words.

As the plants grow, another wire exactly the same is placed approximately 5in. above the first, and the stringing is done as before. So layer upon layer is added as the growth of the plant demands.

16. *Watering during Winter*

WATERING DURING the winter months calls for the utmost care and attention. Needless to say the plants, owing to their inactivity as well as the natural moisture conditions prevailing, do not require much moisture at the roots. Evaporation is very much reduced due to lack of sunshine, and over-watering, coupled with artificial feeding, would produce unnatural growth which would be prone to disease. For these and other reasons, keep your plants very much drier, at the same time, of course, avoiding absolute dryness. The soilball should always be sufficiently moist to maintain that healthy root system, and our 'motto' should always be remembered as well as practised, namely; 'Water if really necessary and leave the plants alone if no water is required'.

A little at a time, as regular as clockwork, is, in all seasons, definitely wrong. When water is given to pots or beds, always give sufficient to penetrate the whole of the soil, but, of course, your drainage must be perfect to allow the surplus water to drain away without hindrance.

17. *Disbudding*

YES, P.F. CARNATION plants should be disbudded regularly. It should be our aim to produce one good bloom per stem, of firm substance and good shape. To achieve this it is necessary to remove, when large enough to handle without causing damage to the main stem, main bud or leaves, all side buds and growth. This should not produce any problems if I give a description as a rough guide, for all varieties do not produce the same type of growth and differ widely in habit.

Disbudding should commence as soon as one can take out the unwanted side buds without causing damage. Often one starts disbudding too soon, being, I suppose, too eager to secure the largest possible blooms by doing so. To remove the buds and unsuitable side growth lower down the main stem is not too difficult, and very little harm can be done if these are removed by pulling them sideways and downwards. It is often with the smaller top buds that serious damage can, and is done. If they are too small to handle nicely, leave them until the next time you come round. It is especially the bud directly under the main bud with which we have to be extraordinary careful, for a slight mistake may damage the top set of leaves and so distort the position of the blooms, which will, through lack of support on one side, be inclined to grow sideways. One could even by mistake not only remove the unwanted side bud but also the main bud itself and so we would have lost a bloom.

One more point about disbudding, and for future flower cutting is also worth making note of, that is: how far down the main stem should one remove all side buds and growth? (See Fig. 10.)

This again differs with nearly every variety. Some produce long stems, others short stems, with cutting-like growth almost under the main bud and very few real side buds.

For cut blooms we must have stems sufficiently long enough, and therefore, with dwarf growing varieties producing only short stems, disbudding should be done to one's own discretion. Often one or even two side growths which would ultimately have produced a good stem and bloom may have to be sacrificed in order to ensure a stem of sufficient length. This is especially the case with varieties of dwarf and compact habit. The Sim varieties, however, produce a fairly long stem, even with the first flush of blooms, and disbudding has to be done to remove all definite side 'buds' and side growth below them if these are of an unsuitable type, being too thin and elongated, and having any appreciable length of stem between the lower set of leaves and the main stem.

As I mentioned before, flower cutting has a close relation to disbudding, in-so-far as where the cut is to be made. It is useless and wrong to make a cut above a joint from which the side bud has already been removed. Normally, each joint or node has one 'eye' and if this has been taken out it would not break any further and so become a dormant piece of wood. I think it would be as well, if I made a special chapter on the cutting of blooms, when reference to this would be in its proper place.

Coming back to disbudding; if we look closely at an almost fully developed flower stem where the main bud is just about to show its colour, and no disbudding has taken place, it will be seen (as is shown in Fig. 10) that directly under the main bud is a tiny set of leaves from whose axil comes a tiny side bud, bedded closely in this joint. Lower down at the next joint, another side bud appears with a slightly longer piece of stalk attaching it to the main stem. The next one again has a much longer stalk attaching it to the main stem. The next one again has a much longer stalk and may even have a small set of leaves of its own, while below this there is either another side bud with two or more sets of leaves, or a sidegrowth resembling a drawn-out cutting with several sets of leaves. This is the general rather than the strict rule. Each variety has its own particular habit of growth. All the buds or growths mentioned so far must be removed either to obtain the length of stem required, or in any case because they would not serve any useful purpose at all. Below the last mentioned growth it is possible to find a good cutting or successive flower shoot, but this can only be decided on the spot. (See Fig. 10.)

I should come back now to the uppermost side bud which we found bedded in the highest joints, directly under the main bud. This bud is partially covered by a small leaf, which does not seem of any importance, but in wrong or careless disbudding, and so damaging or removing it altogether, it is possible to distort the main bud, or cause it to grow one-sided. These two leaves support the main bud, and if this support fails on one side, it tends to grow that way and, at least from the show bench point of view, would be a worthless specimen.

18. *Cutting the Blooms*

CARNATIONS ARE best cut early in the morning rather than at the end of a sunny day. During the darkness of night the plants have recovered from the previous day's transpiration and 'exhaustion' especially if the day has been bright, sunny and warm. In the morning the foliage is turgid and brittle, and the flower stem will easily break at a node dispensing with the use of the knife. I prefer breaking to using a knife, even for cutting of flowers, so that we eliminate the possibility of transferring disease or virus from one plant to another which is a great possibility via the knifeblade.

If, however, a knife must be used do not use it on 'doubtful' plants and see that it is sharp.

Breaking the blooms is obviously done at a node, but when

the blooms are cut, it should be done immediately above and close to a node so that no appreciable length of stem (stub) is left above it. Should this fact be overlooked, it will be seen in time that the large piece above the joint becomes infected with botrytis, a fungus which will grow right through the next joint and, ultimately, may travel right through the stem.

The place at which to sever the bloom we are about to cut was more or less decided when this flower stem was disbudded. It is at, or just above, the node from where the first good side growth springs, which is to provide the succession of blooms later on. I think a look at Fig. 10 will make this clear.

It is interesting to keep a record of the production of each plant or variety, if many plants of one sort are grown. Commercial cut-flower growers do, and it gives them an exact idea of the economic value of each variety. It is often possible to discard the right variety as far as production is concerned, and yet increase the number of plants of a variety which is not nearly so productive. This should not worry an amateur grower who grows strictly for a hobby and pastime, but records do create an interest and much can be learned from them.

The blooms are placed in deep cool water as soon as possible after they have been cut.

The lasting qualities of the blooms will depend on a number of factors, but not the least of them is related very closely by the way the plants have been grown. The more vigorous and properly nourished the plant, the better the lasting qualities of the blooms. The length of time blooms will last when cut depends on the 'starches and sugars' the cell tissues contain. It is these 'starches and sugars' which by the absorption of water are converted into nutrients on which the life of the cut bloom depends. It is for this reason too that it is wise to refreshen the water from time to time but it is no use doing this without cutting from one to two inches of flower stem off each time the water is renewed. The reason is because bacteria will cause the blocking of the water passages of the lower part of the stem causing the water take-up to slow down hence the slow down of conversion of nutrients and the shortening of the life of the cut-bloom.

There are of course various other reasons why perfectly good flowers do not last. There is for instance the stuffy and over-

warm sitting room, which cools off during the night and subjects
the blooms to abnormal temperature fluctuations. During the
evening there is a dense smoke if all members of the family
indulge in smoking. Almost all of us nowadays are blessed
with electricity for lighting and heating; if you should have
gas, you will often have trouble, as cut-blooms and especially
carnations do not like gas at all. This goes too for large quantities of fruit, especially apples, so avoid such conditions as
much as possible so that you may have the best from your
blooms and enjoy them as long as possible. Placing a penny in
the water or an aspirin is of no real value unless it can be
proved that it will prevent bacterial action and life in the water,
which I very much doubt.

19. *Feeding*

IT HAS already been mentioned under previous headings that
carnations, especially those grown in pots, require an occasional artificial feed. One should be careful with this, and wait
until the soilballs in the final pots are well filled with roots, and
the plants themselves begin to show their first flower buds. It
is a mistake to think that a backward or sick-looking plant
can be made to buck up by a dressing of artificial fertiliser.
The opposite may easily result.

I remember a case where a lady had purchased a small
collection of plants from a grower, and after a while found one
looking not quite so good as it should be. She had watered it
freely, so she knew it could not be lack of moisture at the roots.
The plant in the meantime went from 'sick' to 'ill', and in her
desperation she wrote to me sending a few leaves of her plant,
and asked for advice. Of course, just a few withered leaves did
not help to diagnose her trouble, but the wording of her letter
told me all I wanted to know. As a P.S. she wrote: 'I know it
could not be for lack of moisture as I mentioned in the early
part of my letter, and if you were to suggest malnutrition I
could not agree with you either, because I purchased a small
bag of your fertiliser recently, and gave the plant in question

some each morning before watering'. I was inclined to write back: 'Dear Madam, I regret to say that you are killing your plant with kindness'.

Therefore do not over-feed at any time. If a plant does not look vigorous and is not progressing too well, keep it on the dry side for a while, syringe the foliage occasionally with clear water, but do not feed on any account. It is only the healthy and vigorous plants which take the nutrients from the soil which must be replenished by artificial fertilisers from time to time.

Strong and robust plants are a drain on the natural nutrient elements in the soil, and if this is not made good by means of fertilisers, organic matter, etc., the soil will become exhausted. It is not always understood by amateur growers of plants, that one can apply fertilisers to the soil without seeing any effect on the plants. This may be due to a sour soil in which nutrients would not become available to plants. I have already mentioned that plants not doing so well are best left alone for a bit, especially as far as watering and feeding are concerned. Such plants will benefit by being kept on the dry side for a while to aerate the soil. By this I mean that a soil full of moisture cannot contain much air. Imagine for a moment the soil in the pot or beds as minute particles lying closely together, with very small spaces between each other. These spaces are either occupied by water or air. One could go into far more detail in this matter, but this would make the whole issue too complicated. However, if these small spaces are continuously being filled with water, no air is ever admitted to the soil to sweeten it, and the soil becomes sour. Air has the effect of conditioning the soil, and in a soil in this state, roots will form and the plants will thrive. Furthermore, in a very moist soil the plants will not form the roots which take place more freely in a moderately dry soil, where roots will run out to find that moisture necessary to maintain the plant.

On many occasions, I receive letters for my personal attention from past customers who have at one time or other purchased plants from our nursery, and who write that the plants are not doing so well, although they admit that on arrival finer plants could not have been expected. They say that all the lower leaves are dying off, and they cannot think of anything to which this can be attributed. After making further enquiries regarding soil used, how and when the plants were watered, etc., I learn that watering is done each morning before going away for the day on business. In my mind, there is then no doubt at all as to the cause of the trouble. Plants just cannot be watered according to the clock and with such regularity, but as I have so often stressed, only when required.

At our nurseries, we normally commence with the first 'feed' for our young plants some time in August. These plants were propagated during December or early January, potted into 'finals' either in May or June, and by August should have filled the pots with clean roots, and should be showing a number of flower buds. If in doubt, leave the feeding until September, when in nearly all cases the first dressing of an artificial fertiliser may be applied. Manure or soot water, diluted to the colour of weak tea could be given as a liquid feed once every fourteen days, and both will act as a stimulant from which the plants will benefit a good deal.

Chicken or pigeon manure, although very useful, should be used with the utmost care. Both are highly nitrogenous and would tend to produce soft and succulent growth and weaken the plant if not counteracted or balanced by another element. This would make feeding of P.F. Carnations a very complicated business for a beginner, so is best left alone.

Special preparations are easily obtainable from horticultural sundriesmen for feeding plants, but however good such fertilisers may be for lettuce, tomatoes or cabbage, I would not always recommend them for use on carnation plants. Each kind of plant has its own particular requirements, as have animals. For instance, you would not feed a horse or cow on pig swill, although the results obtained in fattening a pig with swill and barley meal are excellent; nor would you place some hay ready for a dog.

For lettuce, for instance, a nitrogenous manure which creates and encourages leaf formation would be ideal, while for beans which are grown for the pods they bear, a phosphatic fertiliser would be better. I do not say that either do not require anything else. All plants need nitrogen(N), phosphate(P), potash(K) and other elements, but some need more of one, while others require more of another. It has also been proved by scientific experiments that some plants prefer nitrogen in the form of dried blood, while others react better to sulphate of ammonia, etc.

The scientists tell us that human beings require a certain number of calories or vitamins per day, and so do pigs, horses, etc. We need proteins, fats, starches and sugar, but a breakfast made up of boiled potatoes as they are lifted from the land, with a dash of cod-liver oil and some barley and maize meal, would hardly be called an appetising breakfast as compared with bacon and eggs. Yet both 'dishes' contain calories, vitamins, proteins, fats, starches and sugar.

I do not think we need go much further as it must be understood by now that we just cannot feed carnation plants with anything we buy in a bag from the garden shop. Always obtain a well-known brand of carnation fertiliser. There are several to be had, but use *strictly* according to maker's direction and do not increase the dosage recommended. Do not imagine, for instance, that you will cut twice as many blooms of double the normal size of flower if you increase the dose. It would be either a waste of fertiliser or, if you overdo it too much and too often, you will cause deterioration of roots and ultimately the collapse of the plant.

Remember, that during summer when watering has to be done frequently, more so with plants in pots and to a lesser extent also with plants in beds, some leaching of plant nutrients is unavoidable and consequently the application of fertiliser must be increased.

Overfeeding, however, leads to dangers too. It results in accumulation of salts in the soil (in technical terms referred to as a low or high pC. value) which causes damage to the finer hair roots, preventing the uptake of water and may, if severe, well cause wilting of the plants. If this should be suspected it is best to water the plants really heavily so that the salts will be brought in solution and leached or washed out of the soil.

During the winter far less feeding is called for, and, depending on prevailing conditions, it could be discontinued during December and January. The temperature in the greenhouse should not be kept too high. During dull days, the boiler can be fired a little harder, but at the same time all possible ventilation should be given.

Extra boiler heat is not required so much to raise the actual temperature in the greenhouse, but to keep the air in the greenhouse drier by a better circulation.

It is possible, that during January or February the plants are not quite as they ought to be owing to the much shorter days and sunless winter weather, coupled perhaps with too high a temperature and, yes, overwatering. The foliage may not have that sturdy appearance of the healthy dark green foliage with that silvery bloom upon it, while the bloom stems cannot support themselves and hang limp over the supports. Such plants have obviously been forced and are best kept a little drier for a time. At the same time improve conditions generally, see that the glass of the greenhouse is clean and ventilate as freely as conditions permit.

If grown well during the winter, the plants should be well and strong and with the approach of better weather, more sunshine and light, they will soon show activity by the production of new growth. Then will be the time to commence with a spring feed. A light dressing of dried blood could be given, which should be followed a fortnight later by a dose of carnation fertiliser. From then onwards feeding the plants in their second year should be done, at first perhaps at intervals of three weeks, later more frequently. During the actual summer months of June, July and August, a weekly application will be required.

Although lime is not actually a fertiliser, I think it wise to mention it under this heading. I could go into great detail regarding liming and the pH value of soils, but it would appear a complicated affair to most amateurs, and is best left for the time being until a sound experience of the cultivation of plants demands a more thorough knowledge on this point.

Let it be sufficient to say that liming is occasionally necessary to sweeten the soil. Lime is also necessary as it assists in the liberation of nutritious elements which otherwise, although present in the soil, would be of no use to the plants. Liming, however, can be overdone; some soils need more lime than others, too much lime content will 'lock up' certain nutritional soil ingredients and withhold them from the plant.

After continual summer watering, the soil tends to become

somewhat sour or stagnant, and during the autumn, therefore, it is wise to give the pots or plants in beds a light dressing of chalk lime. For carnations I always prefer chalk lime as this is milder in its action than, for instance, hydrated lime.

20. *Temperature and Ventilation*

I DO NOT know why, but from conversations overheard, it appears that most people think that carnations are 'hot-house' plants. When I attempt to explain the requirements of the plants regarding heating to some of these people, I find them amazed to hear that we seldom run a higher temperature than 40°F. to grow a crop of carnations during winter, and that it is not rare to grow a house of plants entirely without artificial heat at all. I know that we are very favoured on the south coast, and that we do not often get the severe conditions which are experienced in other parts of the country, where, of course, fire heat is often essential to maintain a temperature above freezing point, but if it is possible to do without, it is sufficient for the well-being of carnation plants. If conditions are very severe in winter, the plants will not come to any harm if a temperature can be maintained just above freezing, say 34 or 35°F.

Carnations love plenty of light, and during winter the glass of the greenhouse should be kept as clean as possible. Even in winter I would continue to ventilate as freely as possible, or as far as conditions outside would allow me to open the ventilators. Do avoid draughts, however, and it may be that you must open only one side of the house and leave the other closed.

Frequent changes of air keep the plants healthy and promote sturdy growth. At the same time, maintain the temperature constantly at 40°F., if necessary with the aid of artificial heating. It is obvious that the quantity of blooms produced will be lower than those grown in a temperature of 60°F., but it has already been mentioned elsewhere that the plants will be much better for this cooler treatment, and higher temperatures would only be worth-while to the commercial cut-flower grower.

At all times avoid fluctuations in temperature, as well as in everything else. Fluctuating conditions are greatly disliked by carnation plants which will show the results in many ways. Split calyx can often be attributed to fluctuating temperatures, or too close an atmosphere.

21. *Insect Control*

THE MAJOR insect pests which attack carnations are, fortunately, fewer than is experienced with many greenhouse crops. However, these few can cause tremendous damage and must therefore not be neglected.

The most common enemies of the carnation are: Greenfly (Aphids), Red-Spider and Thrip. There are also Earwigs, Caterpillars, Tortrix Moths, etc., but the latter are not feared so much as the first three.

I have never yet met a carnation grower who has not been plagued with any of these mentioned, but I hasten to say that with the present-day methods of pest control, they should not cause the headaches they did some years ago.

Controls in the past, particularly of red spider, have been imperfect, with the result that damage was severe and on commercial holdings was sometimes beyond repair. Burning naphthalene on trays suspended above specially designed lamps was about the only way which seemed to give some measure of control but the after-effects on the plants were sometimes equally as disastrous. The plants hardened and this caused the loss of breaks.

Controls have gradually evolved, from syringing with water under high pressure which dislodged the insects and no doubt possibly drowned many of them, but a complete cure or riddance was never possible, to finally the use of powerful poisons discharged from aerosol bombs. Today, control is so much more effective and comparatively simple in its application that there is really no excuse for insects causing serious damage.

In all cases it must be realised that prevention is better than cure and treatment should be commenced at the first sign of the presence of any pest. A regular routine application in order to keep the plants free from any attack is better than to wait until the plants are infested.

A brief life history of each of the major insect pests is given in order that you may better understand their nature and method of control.

Greenfly (*Aphids*). Aphids are small, soft-bodied insects which puncture the foliage and suck out the cell contents, causing discolouration, wilting and distorted growth. If left unmolested they increase rapidly and excrete a sweetish, sticky liquid, or 'honeydew', which attracts ants, wasps, bees and flies, and which serves as a medium for the development of a black sooty fungus. There are many species of aphids but those commonly found on carnations are the green peach aphids.

In this country, it is usually during spring and autumn that we are plagued the most with greenfly. For this reason we make a practice on our own nurseries to start spraying regularly at intervals of fourteen days from March onwards. We may relax a little during June, July and August, but continue normal routine spraying again from the beginning of September until the end of October.

Aphids live in colonies and are at first found on the underside of leaves and on the young terminal growth, the adults give birth to living young and in the greenhouse this method of reproduction may continue throughout the year. Out of doors many species develop females which lay eggs. All the lice hatching from the eggs are females and are capable of producing young without the intervention of the male. The newly born aphids develop very rapidly and are very prolific. A single female may give birth to 100 young at the rate of from four to nine a day. Eggs may overwinter and hatch the following spring.

Fortunately aphids are easily killed. Formerly, some form of nicotine used as a spray or fumigant was a common control. It is still effective today, but plants should not be sprayed during spells of bright sunshine as otherwise the foliage will be 'scorched'. A temperature of 60°F. should be maintained for the best effect. Nicotine (96–98%) is diluted with water at the rate of one ounce of nicotine to ten gallons of water, and if clean rain water is available it is best to use this, as soft water will provide a better coverage of the foliage.

I do not favour the use of soft soaps on carnations as this tends to spoil the 'bloom' on the foliage, which, after frequent spraying with a soapy or oil solution will be damaged. This 'bloom,' is a waxy cover, or natural protection provided for the

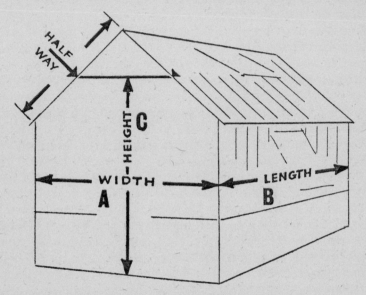

FIG. 13 In order to arrive at the cubic capacity of one's greenhouse, measure as indicated and multiply $A \times B \times C$=cubic capacity

plant. A nicotine spray is best applied in the evening or during a dull day, but always ensure a greenhouse temperature of 60°F.

During prolonged periods of rain, when humidity is already high, and during the winter months (November–February) I would not use a spray at all but rely solely on dusting the plants with an appropriate dust such as D.D.T./Lindane or apply a smoke 'bomb'. The application of a wet spray would increase humidity still further and the plants would not dry very quickly. Damping off would be the result and conditions would be favourable for the development of fungus.

When using smoke 'bombs' I need not stress the importance of a reasonably smoke-proof greenhouse. The size of the smoke bomb is calculated on the cubic capacity of the greenhouse by multiplying length by width by average height (Fig. 13). Large cracks or gaps should be temporarily stopped up to avoid smoke losses during fumigation, and here again the temperature during the process should be not less than 60°F. and if possible it should be increased a little, to as much as 70°F.

Another popular spray is T.E.P.P. (Tetra-Ethyl-Pyro-Phosphate) an improved form of H.E.T.P. It has a great advantage over nicotine as it is fully effective at lower temperatures. It also controls red spider in the adult stages and regular applications will keep the plants free from both pests. Once a T.E.P.P. solution has been mixed it should, however, be used without undue delay as the material soon decomposes when mixed with water. It should not be used as a combined spray with any copper or alkaline solutions, or the effects of the T.E.P.P. would be entirely lost.

Finally, a more recently introduced phosphorous insecticide is 'Metasystox'. This is an insecticide with a truly revolutionary application. It is 'systemic', i.e. it is incorporated in the sap stream of the plant. It is much safer to use than other systemics and can be applied without the troublesome restrictions necessary with most phosphorous insecticides.

Metasystox, however, comes under the Poisonous Substances regulations and should be applied and handled with care.

Metasystox is an ideal material for soil watering. When watered onto the soil it is absorbed by the roots and carried to all parts of the plant. It is applied with the normal watering.

When this material is used, the whole plant becomes poisonous to insects sucking the cell sap. Metasystox is mainly effective against aphids (greenfly) and red spider pests which are often difficult to reach by spraying, dusting or smokes, especially when foliage is damp. Plants watered with this material should remain clear of aphids for something like two months. It is claimed by the manufacturers that freedom from red spider could be even longer.

On carnations the rate of dilution is: 1 fluid ounce of Metasystox to 12½ gallons of water. Young plants, i.e. in their first year, should be watered at the rate of approximately two gallons per sq. yard. Plants in their second year are watered at three gallons per sq. yard. The best results are always obtained where plants are growing freely and growth is vigorous because the uptake of the moisture is greater and more rapid.

Precautions As already mentioned Metasystox is listed under 'Poisons' and care should, of course, be taken. It is advisable to use rubber gloves when mixing the concentrate but protective clothing is not considered necessary when watering. *Metasystox, should never be used on edible crops such as tomatoes, cucumbers, lettuce, cabbage and the like, whether under glass or in the open.*

Red Spider. Red spiders are not spiders but mites and are not always red,but may be greenish, yellow or brown in colour. They are minute insects about one-fiftieth of an inch in length. They puncture the tissues of the foliage and suck out the cell contents. These tiny punctures cause minute white scars on the foliage and the sucking of the cell contents causes the leaves to become dull and to lose their blue-green waxy appearance and instead become dull grey. Eventually the leaves would turn brown. The whole plant would become weakened and stunted, and undoubtedly would die if nothing was done to free the plants from this menace.

In serious attacks, the mites would first appear on the lower mature leaves, a careful examination under a magnifying glass would show them on the underside of the leaves. Masses of small white eggs in large clusters would also be noticed clearly. Before very long, and especially during spells of close warm weather, the entire plant would be covered and the mites would be seen to move busily. They would cover the entire bud and form a web over buds and leaves.

The experienced grower would know at once if his plants were infected by the appearance of the plant, long before he could actually see these minute pests.

The eggs which under the magnifying glass resemble dewdrops, are deposited on the underside and later all over the leaves. In four to five days, minute larvae are hatched from them. These begin feeding at once and continue for about a day, after which they fasten themselves to the leaf and enter a resting stage for another day. The skin is shed and the primary nymph appears. This nymph feeds for a day and then enters a resting period of the same length. The secondary nymph then emerges and follows the same procedure. After the last resting period, the full grown adult female emerges. She feeds for two or three days before laying eggs. At this time, mating and migrating takes place. Eggs are laid at the rate of six a day for the next eight or ten days. The female lives for about two weeks in a high temperature but may live a month at 60°F. Approximately six to eight days are required to complete development from egg to adult.

Adults are difficult to destroy and eggs even more so. After each spraying or fumigation, therefore, there will almost always be some adults and eggs left. The adults will soon produce more eggs and, consequently, if an infestation is heavy at the first start, spraying or fumigating should be continued at five to six day intervals until there are no further signs. A ten to fourteen day application of a control measure would be about right if the plants appear to be free.

Materials used to control red spider are, T.E.P.P. (as for greenfly) and Azobenzene. There are others available for commercial growers, but are not normally obtainable for amateur usage, because they are very poisonous and dangerous. T.E.P.P. as a wet spray and Azobenzene as a smoke are very effective.

The use of T.E.P.P. has already been fully discussed under 'greenfly' and Azobenzene smoke 'bombs' are very simple to use. Again these are calculated according to cubic capacity and each such bomb clearly states the number of cu. ft. of greenhouse space it will cover.

When Azobenzene has been used it may be observed that the 'kill' is not immediate and may take up to seven days. It is possible for the adult female to lay another batch of eggs before it dies and a further application some six or seven days later is essential. A temperature of 60°F. is necessary which should be maintained and, if possible, slightly increased for a period of three hours from the time the bombs are ignited.

It is during periods of thundery, hot, and dry spells that red spiders manifest themselves all over the greenhouse in a very short space of time. It is, therefore, desirable to create conditions which are not favoured by these insects. Damping down the paths and greenhouse floors when the atmosphere is dry and warm is advisable so as to create some humidity in the greenhouse. Shading, and all possible ventilation to keep the temperature down, will also be of great help.

I do not favour, however, continual syringing of the plants themselves, as was nearly always practised in nurseries some years ago. This will give rise to outbreaks of rust and spot as well as encourage botrytis and mildew.

Furthermore, keep your plants vigorous and healthy. It is invariably the poor, weak and undernourished plant which will be the first to be prone to infestation by red spider.

Finally, I suggest again Metasystox as mentioned for greenfly. A systemic insecticide, it remains active for several weeks if watered on to the soil so that the plants absorb it through the roots, whence it will be conveyed to all parts of the plant rendering them more or less proof against the attack by red spider as well as greenfly.

Thrip. There are several species of thrip which attack carnations, but all are similar in habit and in the type of injury caused. They are minute, slender, wormlike insects of not more than one twentyfifth of an inch in length. They move very rapidly and possess two pairs of featherlike wings. They are of many colours but at the adult stage are usually brown. Their mouth structure differs from those of red spider and aphids. First they rasp the surface where they intend to feed and then suck the plant juices. This surface injury is more conspicuous than the puncture inflicted by spiders or aphids. If made on the flower petals, within the unopened flower bud, there will be white marks of irregular size on the flower petals when the bloom opens; if the leaves, or even the stems, are attacked, the rasped surface will heal and leave a brown scab.

Damage is nearly always done before we are aware of their presence and great damage is usually done to the blooms. Because thrips are so completely protected within the flower bud, it is very difficult to reach them with sprays or fumigants.

During the summer, and it seems to coincide with haymaking time, they fly or are blown into the glasshouse, so that even if a satisfactory kill is obtained, another batch is likely to appear within a few days.

We make a practice (I would recommend to everyone who gets troubled with thrip) of dusting the lower parts of the plants and ensuring a reasonable cover over the greenhouse floor, bed or pot surfaces, with D.D.T. 5%. It is necessary to use the 5% version as we have not had satisfactory results with the D.D.T. 2½%. We do this first in April, again in May and finally during the month of June. During July, August and September we dust the entire plant with D.D.T. 2½%.

Nicotine spraying as recommended for greenfly can also be effective, but only against those insects with which actual contact can be made.

Thrips may lay eggs in the leaf tissue, or the females may pierce the buds and lay their eggs within the buds, where they hatch out in about eight days. During the period of development (from ten to twenty days) these larvae enter a resting stage of from four to six days, after which the fully mature adult emerges.

While feeding, the thrip exudes minute drops of reddish fluid which later turns black.

Cuckoo-spit. A widely-known insect which sucks sap from the plant, and belongs to the same group as the greenfly, it exudes a spit-like fluid from its body as a means of protection. We are not nearly so much troubled with this pest today as we were years ago, when it was a most common occurrence to see carnations, even under glass, with this 'spit' on the plants. Inside this mess a round whitish yellow insect may be found; it is not nearly so rapid in its movements as any of the others. Treat as for greenfly, and it should then not be difficult to keep the plants free.

Caterpillars. These do untold damage to almost any part of the plant, but mostly to buds and blooms. They vary in colour and habit a good deal, but all mostly feed at night. It is, therefore, some time after ten p.m. that is the best time to find them at work. By the light of a bright torch it is easy to catch and destroy them.

Sometimes, a few may be found during the hours of daylight but most of them will have withdrawn to the soil where they hide during the day.

An occasional dusting with D.D.T. 5% powder is all that is

necessary; the D.D.T. smoke bombs used for other insect pests will also keep caterpillars at bay.

Earwigs. These are a constant nuisance and cause consider- able damage to blooms. No remedy has as yet been found, and we must continue to trap them in the same way our fathers used to do, namely, stuff flower pots with hay or dry moss, and hang upside down on canes at intervals among the plants. Each morning the hay or moss has to be examined and if earwigs have been troubling you, several are sure to be found sleeping, when it is easy to destroy them.

Although I have not heard any claims by horticultural chemists that D.D.T. will kill earwigs, we have found at our nurseries that plants regularly dusted with this powder were not attacked by earwigs, while plants not so treated were badly infested with them. I think it well worthwhile to make a trial with some D.D.T. 5% powder, should you get trouble with these little creatures, because I assure you they will quickly spoil a nice batch of blooms for you.

Wireworm, Leatherjackets. Wireworms, leatherjackets, symphilids, eelworm as well as a host of minor soil insects can be destroyed by sterilising the soil with steam prior to planting or potting. Soil sterilisation by chemicals such as Novo-Formalde-hyde-Sterizal, etc. will also eradicate these soil borne pests.

None of these are found on the plants as are the previously mentioned insects, but are always in the soil. Wireworm in particular have a natural liking for lettuce, carrots or potatoes, but I am sure that the carnation is their most favourite dish for the damage they can do is very great indeed.

Wireworms bore into the base of the plant, causing the entire plant to collapse in time. It is often in new turf that large numbers may be found, where they are living on the fibre, but once carnations are planted or potted into infested soil, they are given preference, however much fibre there is present in the soil. Where the soil is used in beds, and time permits, it is always wise to bury at various places all along the bed, pieces of carrot, just below the surface and marked with a little stick so that they may easily be found. If one examines the carrot each morning, large numbers of these wireworms may then be caught and destroyed. I have also seen lettuce plants planted between young carnation plants, to act as traps for wireworms, but a piece of carrot is by far the best way.

D.D.T. dust, raked into the soil at the rate of two ounces per square yard, four or five weeks before planting, is another means of clearing the soil of this menace, but the best and most effective method of dealing with them is steam-sterilisation. This is one of the many reasons why we always steam-sterilise large quantities of maiden loam well in advance.

Tortrix. Tortrix caterpillars are yellowish green to olive green (depending on their age) with browning heads. They grow up to about ¾in. long. The adult moth is small with grey-brown forewings and some orange on the hindwings. The larvae do most damage to the tips of the shoots and to the flower buds. The first signs of attack are rolled leaves or tips of shoots spun together in which the caterpillars feed.

To get the best control, treatment should begin early to kill the moths or the young caterpillars before they have spun the leaves together.

A dust to be used to combat this menace is D.D.T. 5%. Repeated applications will be necessary.

D.D.T./Lindane smokes are also very effective but must be repeated at least three times at intervals of fourteen days.

22. *Diseases of Carnations*

UNDER THIS heading we would mention rust and spot although it would be incorrect to call them a disease, in the same way as we understand it in the case of stem-rot and wilts.

Rust. This has been known as long as carnations have been grown by man. Although it can ruin plants, it need not cause a grower fear, as so often is the case. It is caused by a fungus which thrives and spreads under certain conditions, and would disappear if those conditions were altered. Before applying remedies it is necessary to see that the conditions encouraging rust are removed; high humidity, continual overhead spraying and hosing, which causes the plants to remain covered with fine particles of moisture, are all favourable for promoting this disease. If in hot weather, damping down has to be done as advised should red spider be troublesome, do so before noon, or at any rate see that whenever it is done the plants will again be dry before nightfall.

Incorrect feeding or the use of an unbalanced fertiliser could also encourage rust, especially if such fertiliser tends to produce soft and tender growth as would be the case, for example, with nitrogenous fertilisers wrongly used.

Give plenty of ventilation, and keep the beds or pots moderately dry for a while, until improvement is noticeable. As a boy, I can remember asking the foreman once: 'What is the cause of rust?', and his answer was: 'Bad growing, boy!' Many years of practical connections with carnation growing have proved his words to be absolutely correct.

Grow your plants correctly and no rust will trouble you. Here again, as mentioned on more than one occasion in my notes, be observant, and learn to understand the conditions and environments in which a carnation plant thrives, and carnation growing will not be so difficult as at first imagined.

If troubled with rust, spray the plants with Bordeaux mixture, or any coloidal copper spray, but, remember, this would be of no use if the conditions which encouraged this trouble in the first instance were not rectified.

A Zineb spray or dust such as wettable or dry Murphane has been found very effective both against rust as well as spot. Use the wet form as a spray during summer and the dry powder form by means of a good dust blower during autumn and winter. Do it regularly, say, every fourteen days during the latter part of August–September and October, and if plants are clean, continue a monthly dusting throughout the winter as a precautionary measure.

Spot (*Septoria Dianthus*). Appears on the leaves in the form of a circular or slightly oblong spot—hence the name. It is easily distinguished; the centre of the spot is brownish in colour, with a darker ring, often purple, around it. Such spots can sometimes also be found on the stems, but this is not so frequent.

Plants left in the open too long after the summer can often be seen with this trouble. It is caused by similar conditions to rust, when the plants remain in a too-humid and damp atmosphere for a prolonged length of time.

7 (a) Plant soilball ready
for potting-on

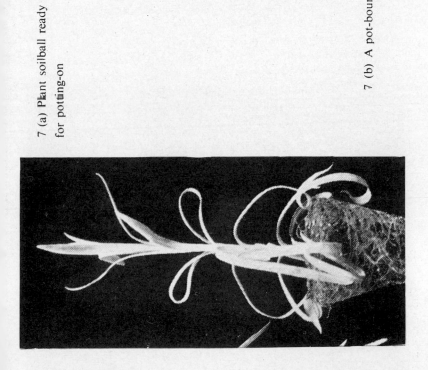

7 (b) A pot-bound plant

8 (a) The first 'stop'. Note the hold and position of second finger ensuring a good clean break at about the 6th pair of leaves

8 (b) A 'stopped and broken' plant

It is wise to house the plants before the cold and damp nights give rise to conditions favourable for spot. Should there be a spot on the plants, dust them with a fungicide powder, after all affected leaves have been cut off and burned. A dusting with lime and sulphur in equal parts is also a good remedy.

Another spot called fairy-ring spot (*Heterosporium Echinulatum*) is not easily distinguished from the former. Light coloured or bleached spots appear on the leaves, stems, and on the calyx. On these spots, rings of black, spore-bearing bodies form. A second row of these spore-bearing bodies develops around the first and this may be repeated several times.

We have found that spraying with a Zineb base fungicide such as Murphane, or dusting with a similar material, is most effective for both types of 'spot'.

Mildew. A white powdery fungus, sometimes found during late summer, especially on buds and leaves, more often than not caused by dry root conditions, but directly the trouble has manifested itself it will spread under favourable conditions.

Dusting with green sulphur and plenty of ventilation, however, should clear the trouble.

Karathane Dust has been used successfully on our own crops these last two years. It is important, however, to dust as a fine fog, avoiding a heavy or uneven deposit on the plants. Apply at ten day intervals always using a perfectly still day.

Alternatively Karathane smoke bombs are obtainable to make the application really simple. These should always be used at intervals of ten days until the trouble has been eradicated.

Stemrot. One of the most dreaded diseases to have worried carnation growers for very many years, is 'stemrot'.

When, some thirty-five years ago, I first came into the serious business of carnation growing as a profession, there was not very much known about this disease. Every plant which died had either a decayed root system, or the base of the plant was diseased. In all cases the trouble was diagnosed as 'stemrot'.

As the disease began to trouble carnation growers the world over, a great deal of research was undertaken in this country, in the U.S.A. and, in fact, wherever carnations were grown.

D

It has been established that there are various types of disease hitherto termed as 'stemrot'.

I feel that the following could be considered a 'disservice' to the prospective carnation grower, as it may create the impression that the culture is accompanied by so many hazards that it is almost condemned to death before it is undertaken. I hope, therefore, that a detailed outline will not be an ultimate discouragement as it is by no means so common an occurrence as it used to be, and besides if one's stock is obtained from a reliable firm where 'culturing' or bacteriological testing is a regular routine practice, the possibility of receiving plants likely to suffer from this kind of trouble is very remote indeed.

The following then will be the diseases which could be classified as 'stemrot'.

Wet Stem Rot (*Rhizoctonia Solani*). Caused by a fungus which inhabits most soil and soil contaminated sand. It attacks a wide range of unrelated plants and is sometimes referred to as 'damping off' fungus. It attacks the plants at soil level, especially if the base is damaged by cultivation around the plants. The foliage becomes dull, losing its green colour. The entire plant wilts suddenly. Affected plants will pull away from the roots at soil level. The stem near the soil is wet and soft, the shredded bark sloughing off from the slightest twist, exposing harder tissues beneath. The roots themselves remain apparently in good condition. Brown knots of fungus mould may be seen about the decayed portion of the stem. The same fungus may also attack cuttings in the propagating bin or pan if the sand is contaminated and soil particles inadvertently find their way into the sand. Dirty seed pans or boxes in which other plants had previously been grown in soil would be a likely cause.

The disease could easily be confused with 'Fusarium Root Rot' or 'Bacterial Wilt'. Only a laboratory test could indicate with certainty which disease was responsible.

Spraying with any kind of material is useless, and effective soil treatment is not possible whilst the soil is occupied by growing plants. Affected plants should be carefully removed and burned immediately.

Bacterial Wilt (*Phytomonas Caryophyllis*). This is a comparatively new disease which closely resembles Rhizoctonia and Fusarium Root Rot. Bacteria enter the plant through the roots. The stem rots at soil level; the plants wilt rapidly. When the bark of the stem is removed, a yellow or brown discolouration may extend up into the branches. The inside of the stem at the soil line is yellow and slimy and fells sticky. The roots also feel sticky; this in both cases is caused by the bacteria.

Maintain the best and cleanest cultural conditions in and around the greenhouse. Again there is no spray which is of any use; no effective control has as yet been discovered.

Fusarium Wilt (*Fusarium Dainthi*). This disease usually begins with wilting of a single branch. The leaves become at first dull green, then yellow and finally, straw coloured. The affected branch dies and shrivels. Infection is at first localised in the stem or branch near the nodes. When such a branch is cut lengthwise, the conducting tissue directly under the bark is found to be yellowish or reddish brown, extending along the sap channel. Later, the brown colour will extend to the inner tissue of the stem as well as into the outer bark from the conductive tissue. When the stem is so affected, the branches on the infected side of the plant will wilt and die. Finally the whole plant will succumb.

The inside tissue of the invaded stem is dry and of a dull brown colour, similar in appearance to dead timber.

It is claimed that protective sprays are used in the U.S.A., some of which we have (with difficulty) imported and tried, but the results have not been very encouraging. To we specialist commercial growers it is well known that frequent claims are made by concerns in the U.S.A. for certain materials or methods which will cure or prevent disease, or again improve culture. By nature, I suppose our American counterparts are more enthusiastic whenever something new is introduced, but, all too frequently such new ideas fall by the wayside and make room for yet further short lived new introductions.

Our nature is of a more cautious kind; not that we are unmindful of the fact that our cultures and control methods cannot be improved, but we are more inclined to make many small scale experiments and only report something really new when something has definitely been proved to do this or that.

I cannot therefore suggest any remedy or cure. The only thing which is certain is that the cleanest and most hygienic growing conditions will prevent trouble.

Obviously one should not propagate cuttings from plants which are likely to be infected or have been grown quite close to infected plants. Pot culture is most likely to confine these diseases to a single plant. Deep potting or planting should *always* be avoided.

Verticilium Cinerescens. Another of the wilt diseases; enters through wounds, root tips and root hairs to attack plants of all ages, causing affected tissues to turn yellow and brown. Its presence is often obscured by the presence of other fungi, which also causes the stem to wilt and die.

If samples from such plants are taken for laboratory test, usually two or three wilts can be isolated, therefore, it is not always possible to determine the primary infection.

The fungi are all more or less soil-born and wilt is more prevalent on soil where carnations have been grown for some years.

The soil, therefore, must be sterilised by steam or chemical means, such as formaldehyde. Cuttings taken from healthy plants should be propagated in clean sand, and the additional precaution of dipping them in a colloidal sulphur solution would be worthwhile.

Overwatering must be avoided as the fungi are favoured by over-moist conditions.

When handling plants for potting or planting care should be taken to avoid causing wounds or cracks to stem or branches, as such wounds provide entry for the fungus.

More could be written about wilts, but all of them are very similar and could not be easily identified without the means of a laboratory. Anyway, the ultimate result of each one is the same and for none of them do we, as yet, know a cure or antidote.

Calyx Splitting. Often looked upon as disease; I can at once ease your mind by assuring you that this is definitely not so. It could be due to many things. Firstly, faulty growing would be one cause. The exact cause of splitting is not precisely known. Many fantastic explanations have been offered. I believe that the causes of splitting are: (1) Inherited characteristics; (2) Poor calyx formation; (3) The increase in the number of petals, which may be influenced by temperature as well as other factors.

The formation of the calyx is a very important part and it is the responsibility of the raiser to take this into account when selecting the parentage for his new crossings.

The calyx should be bell-shaped and have sufficient well-formed brackets to accommodate and support the petals as well as adequate 'spring' to allow for expansion.

An average variety will have from forty to sixty petals, although an occasional non-splitting variety will contain as many as seventy or even more petals. A variety with fewer than fifty petals and which still splits, usually has a weak or poorly formed calyx.

Cool weather will cause an increase in the number of petals, not the following day of course, for the number of petals is established long before the flower opens. A variety which normally has sixty petals may increase to seventy or even eighty petals when subjected to low temperatures. This usually causes splitting. Consequently the autumn and spring are the two seasons when splitting is most severe.

Splitting does not occur for several weeks after the buds have been subjected to low temperatures. It is obvious, therefore, that after August, temperatures must be watched carefully, as during September, when the winter buds are formed during times when temperatures fluctuate violently between day and night this might well be the cause of splitting during November and December. The same applies to spring.

It is also fairly certain that soil fertility and the application of fertilisers have a good deal to do with it. High nitrates have been suspect, and I feel most strongly that feeding in excess, especially with nitrogen, plays a part in increasing the risk of splitting.

After a period of prolonged drought, a heavy watering may cause the calyx to split. Due to lack of moisture at the roots, the plant's tissues tend to harden and mature before their time, and with a sudden heavy watering further development of growth takes place, thus splitting the calyx. Also feeding with an incorrect fertiliser, especially when a heavy crop of blooms is just about to come into flower, could be another reason.

Any fluctuations of temperature, or conditions in general,

can be the cause of excessive splitting of the calyx. There are varieties which nearly always split their calyx at any time of the year, even if growing conditions are perfect; these varieties ought never to have been introduced. No remedy is known, or could be recommended, and only good cultivation, at the same time avoiding fluctuating conditions, can minimise the risk of being bothered with splits.

Curly Tip. Another disorder which really should not be under the heading of 'diseases' at all.

From many growers, amateur as well as some commercial growers, we receive samples of shoots of plants, accompanied by a letter expressing the utmost concern, especially during early spring, about peculiar symptons affecting the growing tips, which curl and become more and more distorted, and usually are interpreted as some form of serious disease.

I can recall one particular instance when the writer was so worried and informed me that a few plants thus affected—'had of course been destroyed at once'—for fear of the other plants in his collection becoming affected.

It was already too late for me to advise against such a drastic and unwarranted step, and by including this brief chapter I hope I shall be able to assure anyone else confronted with this trouble that there is really no need for concern, and that there certainly is no question of disease. The plants will ultimately grow out of it with the approach of better weather and, in particular, better light.

Curly tip is more or less a seasonal occurrence. The first symptoms usually present themselves during periods of low light intensity and low temperatures. (January–March.). It is referred to by some growers as 'spring surge'. The plant wants to grow but poor light and other adverse conditions hamper progress.

The tips of young shoots fail to separate and continuation of growth results in a characteristic curvature (see Plate 13a). As soon as growing conditions improve, i.e. the lengthening of the days, more sunshine and better temperatures, the trouble will disappear. Artificial illumination has been tried but has not proved successful. Carnations do not seem to respond to such treatment as is the case with tomatoes or cucumbers.

On rare occasions we have also noticed this trouble at other times of the year and, in particular, on such varieties as Sim types or those of similar habit, with long and fleshy leaves. It was found to be due to lack of nitrogen.

Undoubtedly, therefore, a nitrogen deficiency may also have a bearing on this disorder.

My recommendations are that in winter the glass of the greenhouse is kept clean, inside as well as outside. Keep the temperature fairly even around 40–45°F.; a higher temperature would force growth and aggravate the trouble.

Should it occur at other times of the year, I would be inclined to suggest an application of a nitrogenous fertiliser, such as nitrate of chalk or dried blood, at the rate of ¼ teaspoon per 6in. or 7in. pot, after the plants have been watered, and the fertiliser afterwards slightly watered in. If curly tip is very serious and persistent during very early spring, a similar application could be tried on a few test plants, but as soon as the trouble is corrected a feed with a general carnation fertiliser should be given.

Virus Diseases. Whilst writing in such detail about diseases, etc., I almost became melancholy myself and frightened about the hazards which confronted me daily. I would like to lighten the mind of my readers by saying that while discussing the various troubles which may arise, it is by no means certain that each and every one will plague you in turn. If that was so, I would just write a brief note and advise you *not* to grow carnations. The only reason why I have endeavoured to describe the pests and diseases is to equip the reader in advance with sufficient warning and knowledge so that many of these troubles can be avoided, as indeed they can be by growing strong and healthy plants and purchasing plants from sources where disease is virtually non-existent and kept at bay.

We are now confronted with the most complex 'disease' if this is the right term. The word 'virus' is derived from the Latin and means 'poison'. It has been used by the medical profession to designate infections and diseases for which there are no known cause. There are many theories as to the cause of virus diseases, but no theory has been proved to the satisfaction of all scientists. Because of this many unknown diseases or symptoms in horticulture are called 'virus' as a quick and easy way out.

During recent years much more notice has been taken of viruses, their particular symptoms, their reaction on the plant, the effect on the blooms, and the effects on the cropping capabilities of the plants. A great deal more has yet to be done.

It is known, however, that a badly affected plant will not crop as well, nor will the quality or the colour of the bloom be as good.

No evidence has been produced which would establish that viruses are carried in the soil, although they may be carried in the plants or in the roots that are left in the soil. However, they must be transmitted mechanically for they cannot move through the soil. The use of a knife when cutting flowers or making cuttings could, therefore, be one of the means of transmission.

It is certain that greenfly transport the virus from plant to plant.

The virus is within the plant, therefore spraying would be of little use even if a spray was known to eliminate virus, but frequent spraying to control aphids (greenfly) would minimise the possibility of transmission.

There are three main viruses recognised today in connection with the culture of carnations. These are: mottle virus, vein mottle and ring spot virus.

The effects of mottle virus on the plant appear to be mild. Faint light and dark green mottling of the leaves is the only indication of the presence of this virus, although it may be that it also affects the rate of rooting of cuttings taken from plants badly infected. Once such young plants are established it will also be found that after stopping they will not 'break' as freely as those plants which come from a less infected stock.

It is not known at present how this particular virus spreads or is transmitted from plant to plant. Carnation mottle virus is widespread and is found wherever carnations are grown. Recent research tests have shown that when literally thousands of plants were tested, all of which came from varying origin, every plant was affected to a greater or lesser degree.

Vein mottle virus is not frequently met with in this country, although in the U.S.A., where I believe it to be known as mosaic virus, it is quite common. As the greenfly is mainly responsible for its spreading, we have found that by careful and timely measures to control this pest, the matter of vein mottle virus is kept under control.

Symptoms consist mainly, as the name would indicate, of a light green mottling of the veins. This is especially noticeable on the calyx. Dark green irregular streaks of the calyx is almost diagnostic for vein mottle. This virus is very common on Sweet Williams in the garden.

Ring spot is most probably the most serious of the three common viruses and, unfortunately, it is also very easily transmitted during the handling of plants. Ring-like light green or yellow markings on the foliage, often with small dead spots, together with distortions and shortening of the leaves indicate the presence of ring spot virus.

It is more than likely that other viruses will be discovered in the near future, as is always the case when vegetatively propagated plants are examined carefully; the surprising thing is that so little is known about virus diseases of so popular a plant as the carnation.

On the credit side it must be said that cuttings from reliable sources, where strict attention is paid to hygiene and selection of plants intended for stock, should be substantially free from virus infection, with perhaps the exception of mottle virus.

So far, only attempts with soil techniques such as heat-therapy and meristem culture have met with success, and these only to a limited extent, in removing ring spot virus, while careful and expert selection by visual means could, in any case, produce and maintain stock free from both this virus and vein-mottle.

I therefore, at least at this present moment, do not yet attach too great an importance to meristem culture as a practical means of erradicating virus.

For practical purposes, therefore, either by the amateur or the commercial carnation grower, I would emphasise the importance of the care in handling plants, the minimum use of a knife, regular and efficient control of insect pests, in particular greenfly, and drastic roguing and selection of stock, free from visible symptoms of virus infection, for the ultimate source of propa-

D*

gating material, offers the best means of maintaining healthy and vigorous plants.

23. *Disease-free Cuttings*
(*Cultured Cuttings*)

DISEASE-FREE cuttings are the real answer to avoid the disappointment of having grown a plant for twelve months only to find that it is infected with some vascular disease and is on its way out, and there is nothing else we can do but to destroy the plant.

I know the amateur, and indeed many of the commercial growers, have not, and cannot have for economic reasons, the facilities which are required for the bacteriological testing of cuttings. It is for this reason that some of the nurseries who specialise in carnations have deemed it necessary to install laboratory equipment. Most, however, have wisely decided that it is far better to discontinue the growing of stock plants and propagating, and now buy each year their entire planting requirements at the time they are needed from a specialist firm, which is specifically equipped to provide large numbers of young plants from cultured stock plants, ready for planting or potting, more or less by a specific date. The whole process of testing of cuttings would take more than a chapter to describe it in detail, and, as I am sure that not many of my readers would contemplate such painstaking, elaborate and costly a venture in order to grow perhaps only twelve, fifty or 100 plants for sheer pleasure, I will only explain the main procedure as a matter of interest, since at some time or another the mention of 'cultured cuttings' or 'double tested' stock will arise, and it is just as well to know a little about what it means and entails.

Absolute hygienic laboratory conditions are necessary. Also sterilising equipment, an incubator chamber where an exact temperature of 72°F. can be maintained, and what is equally essential, at least two painstaking and extremely conscientious workers.

Large numbers of test tubes and racks to hold thirty-six to seventy-two tubes, one bunsen burner, surgical scissors, chloros, distilled water, and a nutrient broth. The latter is made up from tablets supplied by distributors of laboratory equipment, and to which is added the correct proportion of dextrose.

Cuttings are only taken from plants which were tested the previous year and have been grown under the cleanest of nursery conditions, and completely isolated from all other plants on the nursery. This stock is called the 'nucleus' stock.

The cuttings are dipped in a general cleansing liquid and the lower 1 in. to $1\frac{1}{2}$ in. stood in a chloros solution for five minutes. This decontaminates the exterior of the cutting and sterilises the outside bark without affecting the vascular parts.

The second worker handles the test tubes before him, which have been partly filled with the nutrient broth, and which have been sterilised in a special steam sterilising unit, called an 'autoclave', so that no bacteria or bugs could possibly be present inside the test tubes which are all sealed off by means of caps.

These tubes are only opened above the bunsen burner when worker No. 1 cuts five or six segments from the sterile base of the cutting direct into the tube, which is again quickly sealed off and placed, under a number, in a rack provided for this purpose. The actual cutting is afterwards placed in a test tube filled with distilled water, also under number, so that both test tubes can be identified later. The former tubes with the segments are placed in an incubator for seven or eight days, whilst the latter ones holding the corresponding cuttings are placed in a cool room where the temperature is controlled and is maintained at 38°F.

After eight days the laboratory workers will be able to determine if a cutting is free from disease by the symptoms of the segments in the test tube which has been incubated. Perfectly clear broth and clear segments prove that there was no bug or bacteria present, as otherwise these would have developed in the nutrient at the temperature provided for this purpose.

Some tubes may show a thread-like fungal growth coming from one of the segments, or the whole of the nutrient may be cloudy, or indeed discoloured. Sometimes a thick, hard, white furry growth may develop on the surface of the broth which may, in fact, be penicillin. But the only tubes we are interested in are those which are completely clear and therefore are from cuttings which are free from disease.

Only a brief explanation I know, but I am sure it is all you need or wish to know about it. It may be sufficient to know that everything possible is done to ensure that the plants are as free as possible from any vascular trouble.

24. *American Spray Carnations*

THIS BOOK has been devoted entirely to P.F. Carnations, although, as mentioned in my opening remarks, there are other species such as the hardy border carnations, pinks, etc., which have not been dealt with, due, entirely to the fact that they are a different species, not only in the formation, size and type of bloom they produce, but also because they only flower at certain times of the year and have a totally different habit of growth.

The American Spray Carnation, however, is truly perpetual-flowering, i.e. it produces blooms throughout the year, and its habit of growth is identical. It also requires cultural conditions and attention identical to the conventional P.F. Carnations in every detail. In actual fact there is no difference whatsoever to demand that the American Spray Carnation be classified under a separate heading. Yet there is a characteristic which is new and warrants further explanation.

As I have already emphasised, the American Spray Carnation will produce blooms during winter as well as summer. It is therefore justifiable to incorporate this new strain in my book on P.F. Carnations.

Cultural attentions are as described in the various chapters. Propagation, potting, feeding, watering, soil conditions, methods and means of pest and fungi precautions, etc., are applicable in the same way as I have recommended throughout these pages.

What then is so special or what is so different? It will be seen that although each individual bloom is somewhat smaller (seldom more than 2½in. diameter), and perhaps not so full, there is more than one bloom on each flowering stem. This then is the only difference. It is because of this that I think they are so attractive and lend themselves so well for general decorative purposes and make-up work, such as a corsage, a floral bouquet, or for decor which requires lightness and grace. They were described by the raiser as 'charming', and one of the first raised varieties was most aptly named ELEGANCE.

The very first variety which came from an American nursery in Connecticut was, however, the variety EXQUISITE from which ELEGANCE was a sport.

The raiser was Mr. W. Thompson, a well-known grower who has his nurseries in West Hartford, Connecticut. This strain very quickly became popular with the American public and is usually sold in bunches of four to six stems per bunch, often providing a total number of from twenty to thirty blooms. It is not difficult to imagine what an attractive and fascinating vase this would make with which to enhance the appearance of one's lounge or dining table.

At first, and remember that these notes were written in the year 1960, only two varieties were available, those already mentioned, EXQUISITE and ELEGANCE. The former is deep purple magenta, paling towards the petal edge to almost white, whilst the latter is a most attractive rich rosy pink also paling to white at the edge of the petals. Both these varieties are highly perfumed with a delicate old clove fragrance, which has so long been associated with the old clove scented varieties of earlier days.

Since then, we have already established a very interesting 'sport' on our own nurseries which will become available as soon as a sufficient stock has been established, and at the same time more varieties of this strain have been obtained from American sources which will widen the colour range of these carnations, all of which retain this branching habit. We have now for instance, stocks of a bright scarlet, a self pink, pure white and even an attractive self yellow, which, together with the original EXQUISITE and ELEGANCE, provide already an attractive assortment.

Furthermore, it was our immediate aim to speculate on seedling crosses of our own and we anticipate encouraging results in the very near future.

So much for the detail of varieties and colours. Although I

have told you that there is no difference in the way one grows the American Spray varieties, as compared with the conventional sorts, there are, however, two fundamental and important variations.

The first is that the plants are only stopped 'once'. When the plants have been potted from the rooted cutting stage into the first pots, they are stopped by taking out the growing tip exactly the same as advised in Chapter 13, 'first stopping' on page 58. A well-grown and vigorous young plant will produce 'breaks' at each node quite freely. No further stopping is required, as was recommended for other varieties, because this strain will break freely without further stopping and well before the ultimate blooms are ready for cutting.

The next point which constitutes the second variation is 'disbudding'. The American Spray varieties are *not disbudded*. To do so would defeat the object of more than one bloom per stem.

Instead of concentrating on the main bud which, by removal of all side buds appearing on the main stem from the nodes below the terminal bud, produces one large bloom per stem, the terminal or main bud is removed in this instance, leaving all lateral side buds which will, by the time they form and open their blooms more or less simultaneously, also produce small side buds themselves, thus each stem making an attractive spray of from four to six open blooms as well as buds.

These varieties are extremely suitable for pot culture and during our initial experiments when batches of these varieties were grown—two plants in a 7in. pot—we were greatly attracted to them and I could not imagine anything more delightful to have in the amateur greenhouse. I am equally certain of the welcome an occasional bunch brought into the house would receive. I should mention incidentally that the life of these varieties as cut blooms is much longer than the carnation with which we are more acquainted, although it is well known that no flower lasts better when used as a cut bloom for decorating the house.

I, myself, have had fresh cut American Spray Carnation blooms in my lounge for over five weeks, which, I am sure every one will agree, is good value for money.

I suggest that the water is changed once or twice during the week and approximately 1in. to 1½in. is cut from the bottom of each flower stem, which is advisable in the case of nearly all flowers. If my opinion is of any value, I would add that I do not confirm the recommendation of the penny or aspirin in the water. Naturally, like anyone else, I have tried it, but never have I had any cause to make me consider this practice of any real value. This, however, is beside the point.

The half-open buds will open well whilst the stems are in water and when the older blooms are removed after they fade, the newly opened buds will maintain a fresh appearance and prolong the usefulness of the sprays.

I sincerely hope that they will gain in popularity in this country as has been the case in America and will now pass on to my next and final chapter, trusting you are still with me.

25. *Questions so often Asked*

1. *Can P.F. Carnations be grown outside?*
Definitely YES!—during the summer months. At our nurseries in the south-west corner of Hampshire, the climate is extremely suitable and normally the rate of sunshine is high.

If summer weather conditions are favourable, stock plants can be grown outside from the end of June until about the middle of September. When the young plants are given their final potting sometime towards the end of May, they could well be placed in a fairly high cold frame on a bed of ashes (see Fig. 14), or clinker. The lights are kept on for some time and ventilated according to prevailing weather conditions. Towards June the lights are removed altogether and the plants can be grown in the open. Only during periods of bad weather are the lights put on, resting on a temporary structure erected for the purpose of giving adequate headroom for the growing plants. This will protect the plants from excessive rain, while the open sides will permit all possible ventilation and fresh air around the plants.

I know from past experience that there are a few varieties which do not take so kindly to this method, and these are

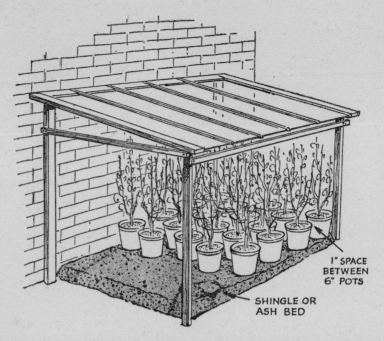

I" SPACE
BETWEEN
6" POTS

SHINGLE OR
ASH BED

Fig. 14 A suitable protection which may be used for P.F. Carnation plants during the summer months, so that the greenhouse can be used for a crop of tomatoes or other plants requiring greenhouse protection

mainly the yellow and apricot varieties. For these sorts we provide greenhouse space. Plants thus grown are much sturdier and provide the best possible cuttings for propagating next winter; besides, for the amateur grower, there is now a possibility of using his small amount of glass for a short crop of tomatoes, cucumbers or suchlike, as long as it can be cleared by the middle of September, so as to house the carnation plants.

We have practised this ourselves during times when glasshouse space was restricted, especially during the latter part of World War II as the production of a tomato crop was more essential in the national interest, and we know that, at least in the southern part of the country it works satisfactorily.

9 (a) The best method of supporting carnation plants in pots. The initial support is by means of a two-legged plant-support before a cane or rod is needed. Thereafter as the plant grows the rod is placed in position and cane-ring supports are added and fixed to the rod as required

9 (b) The end section of a bed showing the end support and cross-bearers to which the wires are fastened and strained. Strings run across the bed twisted around each wire

10 (a) The correct way to disbud is to wait until the side buds are long enough to handle. Remove them by holding the terminal bud and break sideways as shown

10 (b) A typical split calyx being 'rung' by means of a wire calyx ring

11 (a) A dense infestation of Greenfly (Aphids)

11 (b) Red spider mite on carnation

12 (a) Cuckoo-spit

12 (b) Tortrix caterpillar damage to young carnation foliage causing complete distortion as well as damage to the young leaves

Before bringing the carnation plants into the greenhouse again from their outside positions—which should be some time during September, according to outside weather conditions, as by then the nights are becoming much cooler and the general atmosphere is often damp and not suited to carnations—it is absolutely essential to 'spring clean' the whole of the greenhouse thoroughly. Wash all glass inside as well as outside; also the wood and brickwork with a disinfectant, paying proper attention to all cracks and crevices, as it is in these especially that insects hibernate and from whence they will re-appear the following spring. If the greenhouse is provided with benches, clean well under these and remove the ash covering, replacing with new covering material.

The plants themselves, before being housed, should be 'cleaned up' too. Remove all dead leaves, usually found at the base of the plants, make sure they are adequately supported and do any disbudding necessary. A spraying with liver of sulphur and nicotine mixture is advised as this will kill any harmful fungus spores, as well as make certain of the destruction of greenfly, etc.

As each plant has to be handled separately, it is just as well to give them a feed now with a balanced carnation fertiliser, especially one with a fair percentage of potash, but first scurify the surface of the soil in the pot with the blunt end of a wooden label. Once housed, an occasional watering with diluted soot or manure water is of great benefit to the plants. Later a light dressing of wood-ashes will keep growth firm and make up, although in a minute degree, for the lack of sunshine during the duller months of the year shortly to be expected.

A further dressing of carnation fertiliser should be given during late October, and the final one for the year sometime in November. No feeding should be done, at any rate with an artificial fertiliser, during December, January or February. This is a resting period for the plants and the roots are then inactive to a certain extent. Watering is not necessary so often and the nutrients which are held by the soil are therefore not so likely to be washed out.

Remember, after housing the plants, to allow plenty of ventilation as the plants are used to plenty of fresh air around them, and maintain these conditions as far as possible.

2. *How long can I keep my plants in 6in pots?*

To this question I would reply that plants potted into 'finals' (6in. pots), provided a suitable soil mixture has been used and artificial feeding with a dry or liquid carnation fertiliser has been applied, would be quite alright until approximately the following February or March when it would be best to re-pot them into 8in. or 9in. pots in which they could be grown for another year. The same soil mixture as for final potting would answer the purpose. I doubt if many of my readers would care to grow their plants for a third year. Not that a healthy plant would not survive as long as that (I have known plants much older than that), but the present day varieties tend to become too tall so that at the end of the second year they may well be 6ft. or more in height. After that they become unmanageable.

3. *How often should I feed my plants?*

First of all I suggest you refer to paragraph 19, page 70, where feeding of plants is adequately dealt with.

I would emphasise, at the risk of repeating myself later, that it must not be thought that a little from the fertiliser packet works wonders or puts wrongs right. A sick plant most probably is in such condition because there is something wrong with its root system, and adding fertiliser would make matters worse. Correct the soil conditions, and, if after some time the plants respond and recover, it may be then that a very light application of a weak general fertiliser will make all the difference.

4. *Can I grow other plants in my greenhouse alongside carnations?*

Yes, of course you can! Why should this not be possible, provided, of course, you do not choose to have stove plants with your carnations?

It is obvious that a choice must be made amongst plants which thrive under similar conditions as carnations. Summer tomatoes for instance, various kinds of pot plants, chrysanthemums, etc. All such plants enjoy a bouyant free atmosphere, a moderate temperature and free ventilation.

5. *Is it better to keep my plants on staging?*
Whilst the young carnation plants are in pots, even in 6in. pots it is best to have them up on staging. They enjoy the light and obviously there is less chance of draught, besides which the temperature near the floor of the house is coolest. When the plants in 6in. pots begin to elongate it would be better to have them stood on a clinker or shingle base on the greenhouse floor.

6. *Would it be better to use rain-water for watering my plants as I have a large butt in which water from the garage roof as well as from the greenhouse is collected?*
Definitely NO! is the answer to this question. I consider there is nothing else which could lead to trouble more easily.

Have you ever looked in the bottom of such a butt after it has been in use for some months? You will find at least a layer of thick slimy mud which is washed from the roof and contains nothing but harmful bacteria and ultimate sources of disease amongst the plants.

Often too, such water stands in the tubs undisturbed for long periods and becomes stagnant. A green scum will form on the top and in time the spores will grow on the surface of the soil after the plants have been watered from such a supply.

There is no reason at all why I would say that rain-water is better than mains water. All we need is moisture in order to bring the soil nutrient into solution so that the plants will be able to take them up into the plant tissues. Mains water has to be pure and suitable for human consumption and should therefore be equally suitable for the plants.

If you have kept such a water tub at all, my urgent advice is to get rid of it at once and I mean this really seriously. So often I have been called upon to go and have a look at someone's plants as they were not doing well, and more often than not I could not find anything wrong with the way they had been handled and cared for, except that the source of water was from a rain-water butt.

7. *I have an unlimited supply of fowl manure. and find it impossible to get farmyard or stable manure, can I use this in my soil mixture for carnations?*

Only under very exceptional circumstances would I care to use it, even if stable or farmyard manure could not be had. It would be far better to adhere to the John Innes formula, seven parts loam, two parts sand and three parts peat, together with four ozs. J.I. base and three-quarter ozs. chalk lime per bushel, and rely on frequent doses of a liquid fertiliser as a top feed in low concentrations.

One of the main reasons for adding manure is to add humus and this can be done to some extent also by adding peat. The only difference being that plant nutrients must be taken care of separately by means of fertilisers.

Fowl manure makes soils too sticky and spoils the texture, usually it is too high in nitrogen content.

8. *My heating appliance will only give me 40°F. at the best. Will this enable me to grow carnations?*

Most certainly YES! Even if the temperature was to drop to 36 or 38°F. during short periods when outside conditions are severe, your carnation plants would be quite all right. Obviously you would not be able to cut the same number of blooms compared with a constant temperature of 45–50°F. but your plants would not come to any harm at all. In fact, they may well be sturdier during the following spring when plants which have 'enjoyed' a higher temperature may be soft and growth tends to be weak.

It is essential, however, to avoid excess moisture at the roots and greater care and discretion should be exercised in watering.

9. *If I propagate my own or purchase rooted cuttings in January, or alternatively young plants in 3in. pots during April or May, when could I expect my first flowers and how long would I be able to keep such plants?*

This indeed is a long and complicated question. To the first part I would reply that it will to some extent depend on your stopping and when you require your first blooms. A single stop would produce blooms towards the end of July or early August. If the lateral 'breaks' resulting from the 'first' stop were to be stopped again in easy stages up to the end of July, you would not be able to expect any blooms until approximately October/

November. To some extent it depends also on the variety. Some will be early whilst others will be much slower.

The answer to the second part of the question has many ifs and buts. I am sure it would not pay the commercial grower to grow his plants for longer than two years. Some of them do, but I doubt their wisdom and the economics of such practice. The modern varieties tend to become too tall and unmanageable.

I cannot see that the average amateur would gain much by extending it much longer. I consider it by far the best to propagate each winter or purchase a small number of plants in spring, and maintain at all times a number of plants which are in their first year, and an equal number which are beginning their second year.

10. *Is stopping really necessary?*

In order to get the best from the P.F. Carnation it is necessary to stop. It is of course 'possible' to let the single cutting, after having been potted, elongate without being stopped, but as it runs up to bud and flower, the lower portion of the stem would 'harden', become woody and, when finally the one bloom such a cutting would produce is cut, only a few breaks or side shoots would appear from the higher nodes. The bushy habit of the perpetual carnation would virtually be lost and a leggy plant with a low production would be the result.

A 'single' stop, however, is practised by several commercial growers, but usually plants are planted a little closer so as to give an adequate production of blooms per square foot of greenhouse space. Vigorous young plants will produce as many as seven breaks from a single stop. Therefore, seven blooms for certain will be had from this plant more or less during a specific period of from three to six weeks. This may not be desirable in the case of an amateur and I would suggest, therefore, to stop only half the number of leading lateral breaks, whilst the remainder are left to flower. This method will spread to production of blooms over the widest possible length of time.

11. *I pride myself in growing some good quality blooms and would like to try my luck on the show bench. What should I do?*

This not an uncommon remark for me to hear. Frequently, when attending some of our groups at leading shows, we hear such remarks as: 'I grow the same variety and I am sure my blooms are equally as good as those I see here'.

Two years ago at the Chelsea Flower Show an elderly gentleman claimed that his WILLIAM SIM was better than anything he could see anywhere in the show, and, judging from the buttonhole he was wearing, I am sure he must be right. During the conversation I became convinced that he knew his 'onions' as far as carnation growing was concerned, yet he had never shown his blooms. I am sure he did not know what he was missing. I talked with him for some time and did my best to encourage him to take the plunge.

I took him to the Secretary of the British National Carnation Society and after some pursuasion managed to get him to join the society. Since then he has been a regular visitor to the society's shows in the R.H.S. hall, and proved his worth by frequently gaining a First for one of his entries.

Surely there is great satisfaction from growing plants to perfection, but to add showing such specimens to one's hobby is exciting and rewarding. Besides, one meets one's rivals and makes friends, apart from the many friendly chats where experiences and opinions are exchanged.

There is no formality in order to qualify for the show bench. Anyone who considers his blooms good enough can write to any show secretary and ask for a show schedule which will be very gladly forwarded. An entry form will be enclosed and one or more of the many classes are selected according to the varieties one grows.

There will be classes for one bloom in a vase or three or even six blooms of three or more varieties. Complete the entry form and forward it to the secretary who will in time let you know your exhibitor's number. When staging your blooms examine them carefully and stage them to the best advantage. See that the edges of the petals are not damaged and the bloom looks fresh.

A disappointed exhibitor sometimes asks me, 'What could have been wrong with my entry which did not come anywhere.' Well I would not know the answer to that one unless I had been the judge of that particular class.

As one who is called upon frequently to judge commercial as well as amateur classes at shows, I will tell you what judges, and I in particular, look for. I hope this will be a guide to would-be exhibitors.

1. First of all, the entry should be eligible for the class, i.e. a white should be in the class for white, a pale pink in the class for pale pink and so on. If in doubt consult the show superintendent before judging commences. He will be very pleased to help you at all times.

2. If a class is for three blooms in one vase, check the schedule to see if the three blooms should be of one and the same variety, or if it says, three distinct varieties. An entry of three blooms but in two varieties would be disqualified.

3. One of the first points I look for is the back of the bloom. I see to the calyx. If this is split I pass it by and look for an entry which has a sound calyx. Any tendency to split loses several points. The guard petals, which are the most outward petals of the bloom should be flat and in undamaged and fresh condition. So often I see blooms of excellent quality that have been so badly packed and transported that these guard petals have been bruised and show brown or damaged edges. Again several points are lost.

4. Apart from size, the bloom should have substance and form. By substance we mean sufficient petals to fill the bloom without giving a 'cabbagy' appearance. The crown could be high or flat but the form should be even, and the bloom should have developed evenly and not one-sided, so that the petals on one side are fully mature whilst the others are much smaller and give an uneven form.

5. During late summer I often see blooms which have been damaged by 'thrip' (see under insects and pests), which will be liable to point losses, especially if other entries are free from such damage.

6. The stem should be of sufficient length. There is nothing which looks worse to me than a well-formed bloom of good size which is supported on a miserably short stem not more than 12in. or so long. The stem should be strong and straight.

7. Finally, in most classes for carnations, foliage may be used. Do not use fern or any other foliage but carnation 'grass'.

By this is meant a few pieces of carnation stem which have not yet run up to bud. But see to it that such 'grass' is clean and vigorous. There is nothing which puts a judge off more than an entry of good blooms accompanied by thin, anaemic and insect-infested carnation foliage. It would be far better not to use any foliage at all but to support the base of the flower stems by filling the neck of the vase with moss. It is true the judges are not called upon to judge the foliage, but it will not enhance the general appearance if poor foliage accompanies the entry.

I hope that the above remarks will be of some help and encourage *YOU*—TO HAVE A GO!

Time and space only permit me to mention a few of the questions often asked, although there are many more indeed. I hope that the various chapters of this book will help to answer many others which I am not able to deal with now.

26. *General Information*

I AM certain that many readers of my book devoted entirely to the growing of carnations may have been looking, and wondering why, so far, no mention of varieties has been made. The reason is simple; for I sincerely hope that the usefulness of this manual will outlive many of the varieties which are in cultivation today. Since I wrote my first book 'Growing Perpetual-Flowering Carnations' in 1949, many varieties which were popular at that time have been superseded, and of those I would have given special mention at that time, only a few would be grown in 1961.

I cannot resist mentioning, however, the 'famous' variety WILLIAM SIM, which is now already many years old. The constitution of this variety is exceptional and the many sports which originate from it have created a long list of many shades which are becoming more and more difficult to surpass.

The same can be said for many new seedlings derived from a Sim parentage.

I, myself, almost invariably use a Sim as one of the parents of my seedling crosses and some very good varieties have been created. From a commercial aspect I am sure our introduction in 1960, BAILEY'S DELIGHT, is a classical example. It was a cross of Sim Seedling. The new variety produced retained many of the Sim characteristics and the cropping potentials have even surpassed those of the very best Sim sorts.

One of the best guides as to the merits of current carnation varieties of the day would be to consult the awards made to entries in classes at the three carnation shows in London held by the British National Carnation Society each year, and which are reported in the Society's year book annually. This and many other advantages and privileges makes membership well worthwhile.

If at any time various materials, insecticides, fungicides, smokebombs, etc., are difficult to obtain, I suggest a few of the manufacturers who would be co-operative if written to, in suggesting retailers in your area who may be able to help, and supply the items of their manufacture.

Fungicides — Messrs. Pan Britanica Industries Ltd.

Insecticides — Messrs. Murphy Chemicals Ltd., Wheathampstead, Herts.

Smoke-bombs — Messrs. Plant Protection Ltd., Bolton House, 61 Curzon Street, London, W.1.

Dusts — Messrs. Shell Chemical Co., Ltd., 105-109 Strand, London, W.C.2.

Chemical sterilizers — Messrs. Pan Britanica Industries Ltd.

Fertilisers — Messrs. Fisons Ltd.,

Peat — Messrs. Eclipse Peat Co., Ltd., Ashcott, Somerset.

Charcoal — Messrs. Geo. Monro Ltd., Hertford Road, Waltham Cross, Herts.

Glasshouses for   F. Pratten & Co., Ltd.,
     carnations   Midsomer Norton, Bath,
                         Somerset.

Electrical heating   Consult your local Electricity
                         Board (Advisory Dept.)

Although it is generally recognised by growers, I wish to emphasise once more the fact that all varieties of carnations do not perform equally as well in all areas and under all conditions. A variety which does well in the west, may not be as good in the east, and vice versa. Several varieties which I have seen during the years on continental nurseries, and of which stock has been imported and grown on my nurseries in Sway, Hampshire, have been to say the least, very disappointing. Some, however, which have been sent to me by foreign growers and had been reported on somewhat unfavourably, have and some still are, doing extremely well. It should be remembered that each variety is an individual and not all enjoy the same atmospheric and climatic conditions. I remember, for instance, a variety which did extremely well at Sway, namely BAILEY'S SUPERB, a dwarf growing and very prolific variety with large beautiful salmon pink blooms of extraordinary fine shape and form, and was awarded many premier awards as well as the R.H.S. 'First Class Certificate' and the 'Certificate of Distinction' at Aalsmeer in Holland, and yet our stock supplied to the Trial Grounds and Experimental Station in Aalsmeer (Holland) did not gain any points at all during a two-year trial period at that station, and was not recommended. Yet every time we exhibited it against all comers it could not be beaten.

Again, another variety which we raised, BAILEY'S MASTER-PIECE, a large, full-flowered crimson, did not give the same results everywhere. We never had any experience of perfume with its blooms, yet from Northern Ireland and North Wales we received reports that this variety possessed a most beautiful and exceptionally strong 'clove' fragrance.

Local climate, soil, etc., play a very great part in the performance of any variety. The fact that a grower in one area purchased a specific variety from a grower in another area, which did not prove entirely satisfactory, does not necessarily mean that a poor variety was sold.

A few varieties seem to do equally well anywhere and it is our constant aim to produce varieties of this type.

Another point to bear in mind is that it may well be that the second year's crop proves to be much better. When cuttings of such plants are then propagated under local conditions, it could well be that such a variety turns out to be a complete success. However, two full seasons is a sufficient length of time to test any carnation, and if a variety does not prove worthwhile it can be accepted that the locality and conditions are not what this particular sort requires.

27. *Hybridising*

IT IS well known that no two varieties of a species are alike. The difference in habit, general characteristics, form of blooms, etc., are sometimes very obvious. Sometimes the differences are small, but nevertheless are quickly noticeable by an observant grower. The hybridist utilises the variations between varieties and species in his breeding programme, and predetermines plans in order to obtain better types.

Carnations, like other flowers, have both male and female parts collectively in one flower. The male part is the anther which bears the pollen, whilst the female part is the pistil, containing the ovary, style and stigma. Hybridisation calls for the application of viable pollen on to a receptive stigma.

When a stigma is in the condition suitable for pollination it can easily be observed. It becomes 'hairy' and begins to curl at the tip, at the same time it secretes a sticky substance which may not be noticeable without a magnifying glass, however.

When pollen is brought on to such a stigma, either by wind, insects, or by hand, on a camel hair brush, or a piece of blotting paper, it adheres and may germinate, and from there will grow down the style to the ovary. The union in the ovary is called 'fertilisation'. From the combined nuclei arises the embryonic plant.

The planning of breeding in the case of carnations is very complex due to a lack of knowledge of genetics of this particular flower, and even the well-experienced raisers can only be

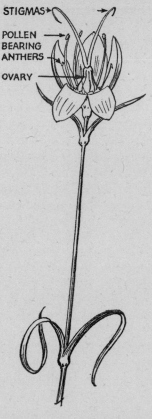

FIG. 15   A carnation bloom with all petals removed, showing the reproduction organs, the ovary, upon successful fertilisation becomes ultimately the seedpod. Pollination is best done in June when the seedpod may be harvested towards the end of August or early September

guided by past and long experience, and rely on judgment rather than knowledge.

Before attempting to 'cross' one should have observed and know intimately the characteristics of the two varieties to be 'mated'. There should always be an aim or object. It could be an improvement of the stem of an otherwise excellent variety. By using the pollen of the variety with the desired colour on to the stigma of the variety which excells itself in regard to its stem, the resultant seedlings *may* have characteristics which combine the two qualities, but I must add a word of caution and emphasise the word 'may'. It is not as easy as it is to write it, for otherwise new varieties and very many new introductions would appear each season.

By interbreeding or 'back' crossing the best of these seedlings to either of the parents it could also be that the desired stem or colour is obtained from the second generation.

In my long experience I have found that there is no hard and fast rule either as to which parent one should use as pollen bearer (male), or the seed bearer (female), as I have so often imagined myself to be at last on the track of something definite, only to find that by using the same technique the following season, the complete opposite was the result.

The chances of producing an outstanding seedling are remote, but there is always that possibility of something exciting. I have had times when I have had three excellent seedlings out of one 'pod', but I cannot count the times that I did not have anything worthwhile even out of 1,000 seedlings.

Nevertheless, even for the enthusiastic amateur there is a lot of pleasure to be had from 'pot-luck' crossing. The procedure has already been described above.

After selecting the parent male and female plants, the bloom to be used to bear the seed (female) must first be 'emasculated'. As soon as the flower is developed the anthers or pollen bearers must be removed—a pair of tweezers would be the best appliance for this purpose—leaving only the pistils. Depending on climatic and prevailing weather conditions, the stigmas will be receptive some two or three days after this operation. The pollen should then be taken from the bloom of the male selected and brought on to the pistils. A warm sunny day should be chosen.

I have already referred to the use of a camel hair brush or a piece of blotting paper.

It should be remembered, however, that each time a cross is made a new piece of blotting paper should be used and in the case of a brush, this should be cleaned after each operation, one cannot always be certain that there is no risk of pollen contamination by pollen from the previously used variety.

A method which overcomes this would be to use a pair of forceps to take out the pollen-laden anther which can then be lightly rubbed over the receptive stigma of the selected and prepared seed-bearing plant.

A matter of a few days later it will be noticed that the bloom petals of the pollinated bloom will have collapsed and are wilting. This is a sign that the pollination has 'taken'. Some three weeks after fertilisation the ovary inside the calyx will have swollen up, and the flower petals will have withered completely. It is now time to remove these altogether and open up the calyx so that the seedpod will be fully exposed to the sunlight. Obviously, a label bearing the date of pollination, and the names of the parent varieties has been attached to the stalk of each pollinated bloom. Such details should also be noted in one's notebook.

Directly the seedpod has turned brown it will be time to harvest. The seed should be very dark brown or black in colour. It is best to store these in an envelope bearing the label or similar identification marks.

Seeds may be sown three or four weeks after gathering or may be stored for some time for sowing at a later date. I always prefer to sow my seed some time during early December so that my first seedling will be coming into bloom by the following June or July.

28. *Soil-less Culture-Hydroponics and Ring Culture*

AT THE time when I had just finished my manuscript and was about to forward it to my publishers, my mail-bag contained a letter asking for details and particulars with reference to 'Ring Culture' as far as carnations are concerned. I realised at once that such enquiries are often before me and I cannot consider my book complete without some reference to, or at least my personal opinion stated upon, this aspect.

By soil-less culture we mean the growing of plants in any media other than soil. We, ourselves, have done a good deal of experimental work, searching first of all for the media which was the most suitable and would give the best results. Our initial start was made in a glasshouse where we had four concrete beds, complete with concrete bottoms. Adequate drainage was provided, and in addition, each bed had a layer of some 2in. of coarse shingle as a base. No. 1 bed was filled with sharp washed sand to a depth of 6in.; No. 2 contained ⅜in. washed shingle only, excluding all traces of sand; No. 3 was filled with a sand and peat mixture in the ratio of 3:1 by volume, whilst No. 4 had our usual soil mixture as already described in an earlier chapter, as the growing media. All beds were planted at the same time with plants identical in every way, each bed containing the same number of plants. Obviously, we were at that time only conducting experiments in order to find out which of these three types of media had anything to offer in advance of the conventional soil mixture. Each bed received the same treatment, such as fertiliser applications, insect and fungi sprays or smokes, etc. The only exception was made in regard to watering, for it was soon found that sand did not dry out as rapidly as we had imagined and at each watering did not require the same amount as was necessary to water the soil bed adequately.

This experiment lasted for the full two-year period and results were certainly of the utmost interest when final comparisons were made. As we expected, the soil bed production coupled with quality of blooms compared more than favourably with our records over the entire nursery, where of course our commercial crops were grown in a more or less identical soil compost. The results were somewhat better, but this was due no doubt to more particular care by our foreman, who, himself, looked after these four beds with the utmost care and concern.

The shingle bed (bed No. 2) was the most disappointing, although during the first six months it was equal to the result recorded for beds 1, 3 and 4.

Bed No. 3, which was filled with the sand/peat mixture, was the best bed from the very start.

Bed No. 1, after a twelve-month period was equal to bed No. 4 (the soil bed), and certainly very much better than bed 2 (shingle) which by now was lagging sadly behind.

The final result could be summed up as follows:

Shingle was not considered a suitable media and production was far less than bed No. 1 or No. 4. The quality of blooms cut was very much below standard.

Sand. Results were encouraging and well in line with those recorded on soil (bed No. 4). Quality of blooms was excellent, although during the last winter period a small number of 'blind' buds were to be found. I was of the opinion that the sand media would be improved by adding a proportion of $\frac{3}{4}$in. washed shingle, and our future experiments should include a trial.

Sand/Peat. This was by far the most outstanding bed, even surpassing the best we had ever obtained anywhere in the nursery. We commenced cutting the first blooms at least three to four weeks earlier than on the soil or sand beds, quality of blooms was slightly better, and growth and flower stems were more vigorous and stronger. It showed great promise. At the end of the first year this bed had produced six and a quarter blooms per plant more than the next best.

This bed was left in two months longer than the other beds and during these two months peculiarities were noted. Some plants lost colour and turned yellowish, whilst others, in particular along the outside of the beds, took on a dull appearance. Sand/peat samples were analysed and tissue analyses were made. It was found that there were 'salt concentrations' which could easily have accounted for these symptoms.

The next two years were devoted to looking for the best sources of nutrients to meet the requirements of carnations. Again, one bed was kept with a soil mixture for control record purposes. The other three beds contained the same mixture of sand and peat at the rate of 3:1 by volume.

All beds, including the soil bed, received the same fertilisers, namely Nitrogen(N), Phosphate(P) and Potash(K), as well as essential trace elements in minute quantities which we made up ourselves. The exception was that each bed had a different concentration, although identical applications were made.

Bed 1 (sand/peat) N3—P1—K1 (high nitrogen)
Bed 2 (sand/peat) N1—P1—K1 (balanced)

13 (a) Curly tip

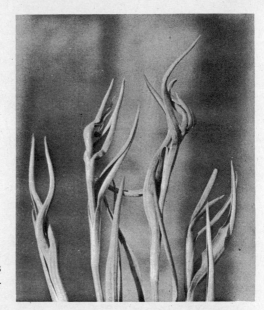

13 (b) Carnation plants
in the foreground severe-
ly affected by 'Wilt'

14 (a) This plant shows obvious signs of rust, a fungus disease which is not easy to diagnose in its early stages. Careful attention to watering and a relatively dry atmosphere will keep the disease in check

14 (b) Thrips can cause this characteristic scarring of bloom tissue. Regular spraying and dusting is necessary to prevent their build-up

Bed 3 (sand/peat) N1—P1—K3 (high potash)
Bed 4 (soil)   N1—P1—K1 (balanced to compare with
                                    bed 2)

For the first two months there was not much difference between beds 1—2—4. Plants in bed 3 were very slow in getting started and, in fact, several plants were lost and had to be replaced. I felt that the potash predominance was too great for young plants, and this also was the case, more or less, with plants in bed 1 when high nitrogen was used.

It was decided to use a balanced fertiliser concentrate until all plants were growing well and this was in every case very satisfactory. After another two months which brought us towards the beginning of May, all beds looked very well and it was then decided to change over to the formulae originally planned for each bed as outlined above. For some time all was well, but it did not take long to find bed No. 2 leaping ahead with bed No. 4 the nearest rival.

Plants in bed 3 were sluggish and growth did not elongate, i.e. space between the nodes was less than on the other beds.

After some six or seven months, I cannot recall the exact time lapse, I remember that the plants in bed No. 1, the high nitrogen, were inclined to be weaker in stem and had a generally softer appearance. This, of course, is what I expected, but it was our intention to find out in practice what would result.

The first blooms were produced on bed No. 2—blooms of excellent quality with strong stiff stem and very fine vigorous foliage. Some four and a half weeks later the first blooms were cut from the soil bed (bed No. 4). Quality in every respect was good, but by that time we had already cut one bloom per plant on average from bed 2. From the commercial point of view, a definite and appreciable advantage.

Towards the autumn of that year, it was becoming very obvious that the high potash concentration produced more disastrous results than high nitrogen, and experiments which followed showed that carnations definitely require a greater amount of nitrogenous fertiliser than has been considered the case in the past, when it was advocated that a good carnation fertiliser should contain a higher percentage of potash than I would recommend today. We believe now, that nitrogen is of

E

greater importance, although we hasten to add that potash in the correct proportion is equally needed.

By the end of the year, not having made, or intended to make any alteration in the nutrient ratio laid down for each bed, the results of bed No. 2 were outstanding. The soil bed, too, was excellent and as we would have expected, bed No. 1 (high nitrogen) was too lush, blooms were large but not full. Bed No. 3 (high potash) was so much behind that we were considering either changing the feed in order to save the plants, or pulling this bed out, as we could not see how these plants could possibly pull through. The fact is that we continued, despite everything else, as before, but it would need more than words to describe the conditions of the plants. Most buds were 'blind' i.e. did not contain flower petals. Those which tended to fill, did not open, and growth in general was 'stunted' almost beyond repair.

At the end of the year our production figures showed the following picture:

Bed No.	Nutrient formulae applied	No. plants	Total Production	1st grade	2nd grade	Split Calyx
1 (Sand & Peat)	High nitrogen N.3-P.1-K.1.	192	2063	1641	422	406
2 (Sand & peat)	Balanced N.1-P.1-K.1	192	3845	3710	135	128
3 (Sand & peat)	High potash N.1-P.1-K.3	192	1022	601	421	492
4 (Soil)	Balanced N.1-P.1-K.1.	192	3072	3011	61	184

N.B. Only marketable blooms were recorded, i.e. suitable for 1st or 2nd grade. During spring of the second year, plant losses due to accidents or bad handling amounted to:
Bed 1 .. 1   Bed 2 .. 5   Bed 3 .. 2.

Subsequent experimental work has shown us that phosphates do not show similar symptoms in cases of excess, as were to be found when either nitrogen or potash were applied in excess to the plants' needs. I would not consider an excess of nitrogen as detrimental as an excess of potash, as long as it is diagnosed in time. One or two heavy leachings of the soil will generally correct such an excess, for nitrogen is readily soluble and can therefore be washed out of the soil. This is not the case with potash, which is more readily 'held' by the soil. The reason, I suppose, why we have not been able to record any appreciable visible sign in regard to deficiencies of phosphates, is because average samples of soil throughout the country show upon analysis that availability of phosphates in soluble form are nearly always satisfactory.

Before passing my final remarks on our experimental research into the most suitable media and the required nutrients, I am sure that almost everyone who has been interested in these reports will want to change over at once to this method of culture, and, at this point, I must admit that I, myself, would be very much inclined to do so, but for the final three or four months of this two-year experimental period. What then makes me hesitate?

I am certain that 'hesitate' is the correct expression, for up to this point we thought 'it was in the bag'. Cropping records were well up in favour of bed 2, and quality left nothing to be desired. The plants were vigorous and bushy up to the end of the summer period, and the foliage throughout the period had retained that beautiful bluish-green and 'sheen' which is always associated with plants grown under ideal conditions and happy in their environment.

It was from September onwards that matters did not go so well. Slowly and gently, but nevertheless to the more discerning eye it was noticeable how the plants in bed No. 2 were slowing-up. Gradually, they refused to break and it was not long before we diagnosed something definitely amiss.

Sand/peat analysis were made, when it was found that salt concentrations had again accumulated in some unaccountable manner. The plants in the soil bed (bed No. 4) were not similarly affected although the same feeding programme had been used throughout. As the weeks went by, the position in bed 2 became worse, and even soil chemists, who had assisted us throughout these trials, could not give any reason, nor any recommendation as to what could be done to overcome the trouble.

For some very unaccountable reason also, some of the plants

here and there, became yellow like straw, which the pathologist could not identify as a disease. I did not myself associate this with disease either, as these plants remained crisp and firm, but lost all green colour. A peculiar happening which I have never experienced in the many years that I have 'lived' with carnations. Nevertheless, a disorder which was serious to say the least.

To summarise, therefore; whilst there are great advantages in soil-less culture under a system which I have just described, it requires constant use of a soil chemist at least to take analyses of the media and prescribe corrections as to nutrients in order to maintain a correct nutrient level. I am sure that this would not be possible in the case of the amateur grower, and, even on the majority of commercial nurseries, it would not warrant the employment of a qualified soil chemist for this purpose.

It is because of these difficulties that I would say, why depart from a well-proved method using conventional materials which we understand far better and which have given excellent results? I would only consider soil-less culture or any other culture using material other than soil, if for some reason or other soil is not available or cannot be used.

Only then would I reconsider my past experiments and be guided by the lessons learned, and most probably grow one year crops only, or take what precautions I could to overcome the previous difficulties experienced.

Frankly I do not consider it an amateur's proposition.

Hydroponics

This, too, has shown results when trials were made in the U.S.A. I doubt if the ultimate outcome showed advantages.

The method was to have tanks filled with water over which young cuttings were 'planted.' The water level almost touched this layer so that the young roots immediately came through and hung into the water below, which was charged with the required plant nutrients. Not having conducted such trials myself, my notes are brief and repeat the reports I received from time to time from United States sources.

It has been claimed that the resulting crops produced well, and that the quality was equal to conventional methods of culture.

This may be so, but it should be remembered that these trials or experiments were conducted by either experimental or research stations, or by one or two large commercial establishments where laboratory facilities as well as a permanent scientific staff were available to make constant checks and nutrient tests.

Obviously, this method became very involved and complex, and although there was great enthusiasm some ten or fifteen years ago, I have heard very little of it during the last five or six years and presume, therefore, that this idea has, like many others, exhausted its usefulness.

The only thing, quite apart from anything scientific, which I never liked was that nothing conveys and distributes disease more rapidly from plant to plant, and indeed throughout an entire greenhouse, than water. So what would happen with a culture, where the roots of many plants are suspended in one large trough of water, in the event of one diseased plant finding its way amongst several thousands?

The same theory frightened me away from the idea held by some growers here, as well as on the continent, where sub-irrigation was employed to maintain moisture in the beds thus abolishing the need for watering by hand.

All beds were connected by means of a pipework valve system to a large container holding many thousands of gallons of water, charged with the necessary nutrients required by the plants. I should explain, of course, that in the centre throughout the length of each bed we had laid a series of 2in. land-drains, to which the pipe system was coupled.

Each time it was necessary to increase the moisture content of the media, which was determined by the interpretation of the tensionmeter reading, water from the large container was pumped through the pipe system into each bed in turn, by means of a manually-operated, small, electric pump. Each bed was controlled by its own inlet or outlet valve, and the water level was allowed to be raised up to a predetermined level at which point an automatic float switch would cut out the pump and stop the flow of water. Directly the water level dropped, the pump would again come into action and thus maintain the required level, until the hand switch was operated and the bed allowed to drain back into the tank. During summer, we usually kept the water level for approximately one hour at a point somewhere 4in. below bed level, which we had found to be adequate, in regard to time and water level, to thoroughly moisten the whole of the growing media, by capillary action.

After a decided lapse of time the water contents of the tank were tested for nutrient contents and any deficiency made good.

But here again, what happens if one plant in one particular bed is affected by disease, not to mention as to who is to decide what is required in order to provide the correct nutrient solution? This obviously brings me back to the need for a qualified soil chemist.

So here again, I am not enthusiastic about hydroponics.

Ring Culture

There remains 'Ring Culture', which, although not really classified as soil-less, has been interesting some of the amateur growers of carnations.

Here again, whilst it holds possibilities, and has been proved beneficial for crops such as chrysanthemums and especially for tomatoes, I doubt the wisdom of recommending this method for carnations, and certainly not for the amateur—whose plants are best kept 'mobile', meaning, of course, grown in pots, so that it will always be advantageous in order to make the best possible use of limited glasshouse space.

The system calls for the provision of a more or less water-tight base or shallow trough, which is filled to a depth of 2in. or 3in. with washed clinker, ashes or shingle on to which are placed pots without bottoms. Hence the term 'Ring' culture. These pots or rings are filled with soil into which the plants are planted. For a time, watering is done as usual until the plants' roots have permeated into the ash or clinker base. From then onwards, the roots will obtain their moisture and nutrient requirements from this base.

It is claimed that the plants develop a better root system, and this I well believe, but I have not yet seen any carnation plants which have surpassed the crops grown either in 6in. or 7in. pots or in beds, and attended to by an experienced and painstaking grower.

Once again, I come back to the possibility of disease, which in this method will surely spread equally as rapidly through an ash or clinker base saturated with moisture, which is an ideal environment for any disease.

As I have said before, it is obvious that such plants become permanent occupants of the allotted space. It is true that plants in beds are also permanent, but it is only the amateur with a large collection who would decide on devoting the entire glasshouse to carnation bed culture.

In conclusion, let me say that, so far, none of these techniques appeal to me as a carnation grower, and would not be recommended by me if my advice was sought.

29. *Cultural Attentions Month by Month*

January is the best month for propagating for those who have only a small number to do. Those with larger collections to maintain will have started earlier.

Plants in final pots should have some attention. Dead and old leaves should be removed, and the soil surface should be scurified. Watering of these plants must be done with the utmost care; avoid over-watering, especially this time of the year.

Houses containing flowering plants should be ventilated as freely as outside weather conditions permit.

The days are beginning to lengthen and more light will stimulate more and better growth. We can usually also anticipate more frost, and attention should be paid to boiler or heating appliances so as to avoid low temperatures.

Compost for subsequent potting operations should be mixed in advance and kept under cover.

Seeds sown in December will need 'pricking off' into boxes or seed pans approximately 1in. to 2in. apart.

February. There will be an even greater increase in the hours of daylight and although frosts may be heavy this month, gradually the sun will gain in power, and provide more suitable conditions in the greenhouse. Plants will show signs of new growth. Ventilation during daytime should be increased according to prevailing conditions.

Cuttings propagated early January will be ready for removing from the sand after approximately four weeks from date of insertion, and should be potted-on into 2in. pots, using No. 1 potting soil.

Flowering plants will benefit from a light dressing of chalk lime. Occasional spraying on suitable days will keep the plants free from insect troubles, especially greenfly, which at this time of year will soon make its appearance and become rather troublesome.

Cuttings propagated earlier—for instance, December or late November—will by now have rooted through nicely in their 2in. pots, and to avoid them becoming potbound, keep a careful eye on the amount of root developing in this small pot. Pot them on into 3½in. pots as soon as the 2in. soilball is becoming well filled with roots.

For later applications of sprays and smokes to combat any infestations of pests, make sure you have sufficient insecticides etc. by you, to enable you to control them at the first signs.

If you intend to grow your plants in beds, commence the preparation of these in good time, in readiness for planting.

March. I do not recommend propagating later than the end of this month, so if you have any batches or varieties which are not up to the required number, do not delay inserting a few more cuttings during the first week of this month. Cuttings propagated later than March would not produce the best type of plant to give a good crop of blooms during the coming winter.

Carnations to be grown in beds should now be planted out into their final positions. Distance apart, and other planting details, are to be found under the appropriate headings.

Flowering plants in pots, as well as beds, should have a light dressing of dried blood, to be followed by a good carnation top-dress manure (see 'Feeding'). Plants potted during January, or early February, will now be ready for potting-on into 3½in. pots.

First stopping should be given to plants in need of this (see 'Stopping' notes). As the weather improves, increase daily ventilation, and if possible leave a little air on at night, but at the same time do not overlook the possibilities of night frosts.

Watering should require more attention. The plants will need more during bright, sunny weather, less, in cloudy, dull periods.

Continue your watch for insect infestation especially aphids (greenfly) and spray periodically as a preventive measure.

April. Potting-on should be done when plants in 2in. pots are well rooted through. With improvement in the weather and general conditions normally expected at this time of the year, it will be found that plants require more water, especially those in large pots.

Earlier potted plants, now well rooted through in the 3½ in. pots and forming nice breaks at every joint after the first stopping, can be potted-on into finals, i.e. 6in. or 7in. pots.

One-year-old flowering plants, those which were propagated the previous year and have been over-wintered in the large pots, should now be potted-on into 9in. pots. The same soil mixture as for final potting would be in order. Regular feeding of older plants is necessary.

Growth of plants will become more rapid now, and dis-budding will be necessary more frequently. Go over the plants each week, and remove all unwanted side buds and growth.

Plants potted this season in final pots will soon require second stopping, but do not be too hasty with this. Wait until the shoots to be stopped attain sufficient length, some 9in. to 10in., and remove the growing tip (as directed under 'Stopping').

Further batches of plants now rooted through in 3½in. pots will again require potting-on into finals.

May. Towards the end of this month, plants could be placed in cold frames which are covered with lights at night, but, during favourable weather, are opened up during daytime.

Keep up regular insecticidal spraying. During hot weather, damp down all paths in the greenhouse as well as under stagings, to avoid favourable conditions for red spider infestations.

No more fire-heat should be necessary, in fact, very often

the boiler, or any other method used for heating the greenhouse during winter, has been discontinued for some weeks, depending on prevailing weather conditions. Boilers should be thoroughly cleaned out, removing all unburnt fire ashes; flues should also be cleaned, and the boiler itself should be washed out by means of a hose pipe. Dampers, flue doors, etc., should be left open while boilers are not in use. Door hinges, and all movable parts, such as flue damper regulators, should be oiled to prevent them rusting, and to avoid difficulty next season when perhaps the door may be found rusted up and difficult to open or close. All other metal parts of the boiler could be painted with a rust preventive paint.

June. By about the middle of June, most plants will need some form of support, *two-legged support*. Our speciality is ideal as the first, but earlier potted plants now having had a second stop, will need a second, or even perhaps a third support, and a cane or rod has to be used, with a *cane-ring* support (see chapter on the supporting of plants).

Plants in their second year should be fed regularly. An occasional watering with diluted manure, or soot water, as directed under 'Feeding', is of great benefit. Plants potted into 'Finals' this year, however, should not be fed with artificial fertilisers, but a watering with weak manure, or soot water, can be given from time to time.

During June the first signs of red spider are usually noticed and a sharp look-out must be kept for them. Do not encourage this pest by conditions favourable to it; damp down all paths etc., avoid too dry an atmosphere, ventilate freely and, if necessary, shade the house with a thin coating of whiting on the exterior. This shading will prevent the undue fading of some varieties which easily lose their colour during bright weather. If red spider has been seen, spray at once with H.E.T.P. solution, or apply an Azobenzine smoke-generator.

Further second-stopping of some plants may be necessary, but for autumn blooms, do not stop later than the end of this month.

The summer show of the British National Carnation Society is usually held in July in the R.H.S. hall, London. Do not hesitate to send the Secretary your entry form, even if you have not shown before. If you can manage to go yourself to enter your classes for this first ever entry, ask the Secretary to put you in touch with someone with experience, as I am certain that there will always be somebody available eager to help you to stage your blooms to the best advantage.

June and July may be the best for pollinating blooms intended for producing seed. (See chapter 27.)

July. From now onwards, regular routine work will be necessary. Watering, feeding, supporting and disbudding of plants in flower, as required, will all need regular attention.

For blooms wanted during next winter, this is the last month for the second stop. No more stopping should take place after the end of this month.

Free ventilation with all possible side lights open, as well as doors, should be given; it may even be possible to maintain side ventilation, as well as top, during warm nights.

Do not forget the fact that carnations in their final pots can easily be grown outside, either stood on a thick bed of ashes, or partly sunk into the ground. The latter way will definitely help to prevent excessive drying out. During spells of hot weather, see that the shading is adequate—it may have been removed by a recent shower.

This month there will be a great influx of disbudding. Get it done on every possible occasion, especially if you are fortunate enough to be able to look forward to your annual holiday. Once disbudding and such jobs get behind, it will be difficult to catch up. Also in preparation for the holiday absence, arrange with some kind and understanding neighbour to do a little watering for you and to open the ventilators. Get him to come in once or twice beforehand when you see to the watering so that he will know better what is required of him. I am sure it will help him no end, and you will be in a much better frame of mind when you are away.

Remember the summer show in London held by the British National Carnation Society and do send your entry even if you cannot be there yourself.

August. A light top dressing of a good carnation manure could now be applied to plants potted early in the year into finals. They will by now have rooted well through the soil in the pot, and should be showing their first flower stems, with, perhaps, one or two small buds.

Nothing more than the usual work is necessary. Support your plants adequately by adding, as required, another *cane-ring* support above the previous one; regular feeding of older plants should not be neglected.

Gardeners in the north, or particularly cold districts, will have to be in advance of those in the south, and may have to couple the recommendations for September with those of this month.

Continue your look out for red spider and aphids, as well as thrip. Spray or smoke as suggested under the chapter for 'Insects' in particular the red spider menace. This can be very severe during August if the weather is close and warm. Renew the shading if this should have been washed off and the weather is very bright and sunny.

September. Days will be becoming shorter now, and nights, towards the end of the month, will gradually be cooler and damper; dew is often seen in the early morning. Should this be the case, it will be time to house all plants still outside. Do not do this in too much of a hurry, but prepare well in advance. Give the house in which the plants are to be placed, a good clean-up; also clean the plants themselves, and prepare them for housing.

Plants potted this year into final pots, should now be fed, and the earlier potted ones, fed for the first time last month, should have a second application sometime this month.

Last year's plants, now in 9in. pots, must be kept clean, and if not specially required for flowering, could be stopped down in the early part of the month when, during the coming winter, they will produce an abundance of good cuttings.

When housing the plants, remember that perhaps you will be using some of them for propagation, and with this in mind it is as well to select the best, most vigorous and clean plants, to set aside for that purpose.

Should the weather still be warm, so that damping down of paths is still necessary, do so before noon now, in order that conditions inside the greenhouse are dry again by night.

We send out in 5in. fibre terra-cotta pots, plants propagated during December and January, and undoubtedly this is the best month to acquire such stock.

Lift fibrous maiden loam, and stack, grass downwards, with alternative layers of manure, together with a sprinkle of bone-meal and chalk lime, for use next potting season. Select the best possible soil, and see that there is plenty of fibre which, when rotted down well, will make ideal soil for carnation work.

Sterilize empty pots, boxes etc., which will be required next season, with formaldehyde to allow plenty of time for this important operation.

It will now be time to gather the seed pods from the June/July pollinations.

Watering and ventilation will require greater care from now on. Heating apparatus needs to be looked over during the early part of the month and it may be as well to try it out for a day to make certain everything is in good order. We may have to start a little artificial heat sometime this month, if only to dry the atmosphere which in September often becomes very humid.

October. Towards the middle or end of this month it may be necessary to re-light the boiler, or apply other means of heating to our greenhouse. It will entirely depend on the locality, and if good weather is experienced in the southern part of the country, it is possible to do without fire heat for some time yet. In any case, it is as well to prepare, if not re-light. See that all pipes of the hot-water system are full of water and that there is no air-lock. If the system is supplied with a ball-valve cistern, see that the valve is working properly.

Maintain, as far as possible, a night temperature of 45°F. although we may have started to use artificial heat, continue with ventilation as freely as possible. During some periods of the day, even side ventilation may still be required.

It would now be better to use insecticidal and fungicidal dusts, or smokes, rather than wet sprays. Nicotine fumigating shreds are now preferred to nicotine sprays. Should we still use sprays, it will be found much more difficult to have the plants dry by night time, and rust may thereby be encouraged. Go sparingly with fertilisers. A dressing of wood ashes or ashes from the garden bonfire where hedge trimmings, etc., have been burned, is beneficial to the plants, owing to its slight potash content.

November. If the heating has been turned on, take care not to run an unduly high temperature, continue to ventilate as freely as conditions permit.

In the north, propagation could now start. Days now are usually dreary and winter is almost upon us. Growth tends to become more and more slow, and consequently watering must be done according to needs, and much more care and attention should now be paid to this. Do avoid high temperatures; 40–45°F. is quite sufficient.

Make sure all glass of the greenhouse is clean, and if necessary, wash with a stiff brush to admit all possible light.

Thoughts should now be given to supplies of potting soils, etc. This should already have been stacked, and have had at least one turning since stacking. It should now be brought under cover, because once wet, it will take a long time to dry sufficiently to be of use for potting. During spare time, wash all pots to be used next January or later. Propagating pans, etc., should also be cleaned. A good, sharp sand for propagating purposes should be secured, and our propagating bin may require some minor overhaul.

December. In the south we could now start with propagating, and continue until March if necessary. Potting soils should by now have been mixed and be ready for use. Take care that such soils do not dry out too much; it is best to keep the heaps covered with a damp bag or so.

Occasional handling of plants in 6in. pots is beneficial in more ways than one. By doing so, they will from time to time be turned, so that the part which was at first facing south is now turned towards the north. At the same time, the soil can be scurified, as well as limed, or dressed with a fertiliser as required. Dead leaves etc., could be removed when handling the plants for one or other purpose.

Selection of cuttings is of the utmost importance. Remember that next year's results will depend on your efforts now, and that pains taken in the most careful selection of the best cuttings from the already-selected stock plant will be rewarded by the production of a clean and healthy succession of carnation plants. An inferior cutting cannot be expected to produce the best possible result however good your further attentions may be. Even if cuttings, as may be the case on some varieties, are not plentiful, it would be unwise to take whatever is going; it is better to wait a few weeks and then take some really good cuttings.

When ordering young plants or rooted cuttings to supplement your collection with something new, do so only from a well-known and reliable firm.

Remember too that for many reasons a good, selected stock of carnation plants cannot be expected to be 'cheap'. The cost of maintaining a first-class stock is very great. Should you be led into purchasing plants, by lower price quotations, it will in the end prove to be more than expensive. Invariably, a 'cheap' article is, in the long run, dear; this is true with carnations more than anything else.

30. *My Final Remarks*

GREAT satisfaction and unlimited pleasure can be had from growing P.F. Carnation plants which bloom all the year round. They will commence to produce their first flowers approximately seven to eight months after propagation and continue for two or more years. In fact, they will continue for many years, if looked after really well, until they die of old age. As a boy, I was working on a Dutch nursery where they had a bed of carnations which was then seven years old—I believe it was the old variety ENCHANTRESS. It was not considered a commercial proposition, but it was carried out as an experiment to see how long a carnation plant would continue to produce its blooms.

During the summer these plants were cut back, when they would form new breaks from lower down, and so supply new flowering shoots during the next winter. I remember that the quality of the flowers was all but good, and I think that most blooms found their way on to the street market.

Now do not think that the time from propagating until cutting one's first bloom is a time of boredom, or uninteresting. To my mind, as a grower, it is the most interesting part of carnation growing. To build up a plant, from the young, unrooted cuttings some 4–6in. long, to a plant often reaching seven feet in height in the second year of growth, is by no means boring. There is the continual watch for insect plagues, and mastering them one by one, potting-on, stopping, and seeing that the plants form their breaks, then preparing the final potting soil or the beds. It is a lot of work, but to anyone interested, it can be real enjoyment all the time.

A lot of common sense is needed, and the details in cultivation will come as experience is gained by real and constant observations.

It has been a pleasure to write on the culture of the flower which for many years now has given me so much joy and pleasure. Nothing has interested me so much since my schooldays, as this particular plant, and I hope sincerely that by writing this little book I have given confidence to many, and have given that inspiration to 'have a go' and at the same time, removed that often-heard phrase, 'I would very much like to have a few of those plants in my greenhouse, but then, what do I know about carnation growing?' That carnation growing is so difficult is untrue; it can be accomplished by anyone, provided they have sufficient interest.

To those starting, I wish them the best of luck. May you obtain as much thrill and satisfaction as I did some thirty or more years ago, when I expected my first plant to burst into bloom—which, although not perfect in every respect, gave me encouragement to continue trying and do better next time. It is this which has kept me occupied so many years, as it still does today.

Printed in Great Britain
by The Press at Coombelands Ltd., Addlestone, Surrey